Kasi,

Leah had great ...
with you :-

THE GIFT OF
GREAT SORROW

May you continue to
live your life with
purpose

Louise ♥

THE GIFT OF GREAT SORROW

A Journey Thru Pain to Purpose

LOUISE BRAÜN FRANK

atmosphere press

Published by Atmosphere Press

Frank Publishing, LLC

Cover design by Matthew Fielder

Cover photo: Louise carrying Leah's ashes on the Camino de Santiago, Spain

atmospherepress.com

Frank Publishing: www.joythrutears.foundation
Email: louise.frank@joythrutears.foundation

To my beautiful and courageous children, Joshua James Chalcraft and Leah Ann Chalcraft. You continue to be my guiding light, directing my footsteps, and giving my life purpose every day.

CONTENTS

PREFACE

"We are not meant to stay wounded. We are supposed to move through our tragedies and challenges and help each other move through them. By remaining stuck in the power of our wounds, we block our own transformation. We overlook the greater gifts inherent in our wounds – the strength to overcome them and the lessons we receive from them. Wounds are the means through which we enter the hearts of other people. They are meant to teach us to become compassionate and wise."
—Caroline Myss

Loss comes in many colors. It can come with the loss of a parent, life partner, friend, marriage, beloved furry friend, an ability, a job, or even the loss of innocence. It can also come in what many consider the most devastating loss of all...the loss of a child. In my case, it came in the loss of *both* of my children. Joshua James Chalcraft, whose smile would light up a room, died when he was 23. His sister Leah Ann, my little fireball filled with compassion, died just a few years later at 25. My children suffered and passed from the same disorder, Friedreich's Ataxia, a hereditary disease that lay hidden somewhere in the DNA of their father's and my distant past, unknown to either of us. It skipped many generations before bursting into our lives without warning. Joshua was diagnosed at the age of six and the day my little girl was diagnosed was the day I stopped praying. I had other work to do, to re-edit a life I never imagined could be possible.

I never asked "why?" The only question I asked was "how?" How could I be a great mother to my babies? How could I be the mother they will need? How could I help them find purpose in their lives and guide them through this debilitating disease. And the obvious, inevitable, and most frightening question of all...how would I be able to survive the pain of watching their lives diminish, cruelly cut so short, and survive the agony of losing both of them?

Fortunately my father spoke seven words to me after my children were diagnosed, which set in motion the way I would live each day. He said:

"Watch them live...don't watch them die."

That is what I did. I gave Joshua and Leah the absolute best life I could. We lived fully even knowing an early end was coming. Against all the odds of how a parent might survive the deaths of their children and keep living, I did. I kept standing and even thriving in the wake of losing them. In the years following their deaths, I discovered while I was helping them find purpose, they were giving me the gift of finding my own purpose in life. Watching their courage and strength amid terrible challenges and pain made me stronger and gave me courage I never knew I possessed.

Over the past eight years I have endeavored to harness all the sadness and grief and repurpose it into finding ways to impact others.

Many friends over the years have encouraged me to share my story. This book is my best effort to do just that and unwrap the gifts my children gave me. Joshua and Leah made an indelible difference in my life, and it is my deepest hope, in sharing our story, that their gifts may make a difference in yours as well.

PART ONE

CHAPTER 1

Blood and Gravel

> "Your life is written in indelible ink. There's no going back to erase the past, tweak your mistakes, or fill in missed opportunities. When the moment's over, your fate is sealed. But if you look closer, you notice the ink never really dries on any of your experiences. They can change their meaning the longer you look at them."
> —Klexos

Over the years, so many people have told me they were amazed by how I endured the loss of both my children as well as the years of caregiving for them as their health and physical capacities declined. How did you do it, they wondered. How did you survive that experience, and how can you be thriving so well now? Well, of course it was never as easy as people thought it was. There were many moments of wrenching, unimaginable pain. But when I think of what helped me meet this challenge and what ultimately gave me the capacity to survive and continue to live my life so fully, I have to go back to what happened to me as a child.

I grew up in a very boisterous, fun-loving, affectionate, French-Canadian family. We hugged and touched, and it was, for the most part, a happy loving childhood with many expressions of love. There are, however, particular memories that shaped the mother and caregiver I would become. I was five, on my way to kindergarten, riding along a rocky road covered in gravel. I was just a beginner on my bike when I took a terrible fall. Gravel was embedded in my knee and blood poured down my leg as I ran home to my mother, scared and crying. A mess, I needed to be comforted, cleaned up, and hugged. My mother washed off the gravel, wiped away the blood, and put a Band-Aid over the wound. She said it was nothing and her only words to me were, "You'll be fine."

The other unspoken messages I heard were, "Don't feel pain, just talk about the good stuff, talking about what you're feeling won't make it better." She attached little importance to the external injury and none to what I might be feeling inside. She sent me back to school. It was the first moment in my young life when I felt insignificant, unimportant, and unnoticed.

I would never forget the physical and emotional hurt of that "blood and gravel" moment and I would never forget the lesson that things would be okay. What's a scraped knee in the greater scheme of things? I was not the baby anymore. To my mother, it was nothing. It was time to grow up and toughen up. In time, the wound on my knee healed, but the damage inside remained. "You'll be fine. Just pick yourself up and get back to school." Later I realized that "you'll be fine" was good wisdom to trust but on the other hand, "only talk about the good stuff and not the bad" also became problematic in my life and marriage.

As if crashing on my bike was not enough to garner sympathy from my parents, at eight, I unwittingly and, I think, unintentionally, tried again. I jumped headfirst from my bedroom dresser into my "imaginary pool" which, in reality, was a hard mattress. I heard my neck crack and doubled over, unable to breathe. After what seemed like an eternity, I was finally able to breathe a little air into my lungs. My terrified girlfriend who was with me ran to find my mother who was visiting with her friends at a neighbor's house. My mother stayed where she was and, still barely able to breathe, I stumbled over to find her. She seemed remarkably unconcerned, walked me home, and told me just to lie on the couch. I was never taken to the hospital or even to a doctor. I could barely walk without pain and, while I got to stay home from school for a few days, it took several months before I was able to stand up without pain. I was helped to walk around the house and fed, but received little or no emotional support or sympathy, which made me hurt even more inside.

Looking back on these memories, I now realize my mother came from a family that chose not to talk about their pain, worries, or problems. She lived through the Depression, and everyone was suffering. She was the fifth of 12 children and there was little time or tolerance for complaining. My mother learned at her own tender age that emotions were best left unexpressed. Her own mother died when she was only 10, and she was not allowed to see her to say goodbye. In the wake of her own mother's death, she was forced to quit school in the eighth grade to stay home and help care for her brothers and sisters. There was, she would tell me years later, so much work to do and little time for emotional expression. She had no time for empathy or expressing her feelings. She was tough and resilient as a child and expected her own children to be tough and resilient.

The final indignation from my childhood memories happened during a move to our new home in Quebec in 1968. I was 11. We stopped for the night, camping on our way to Chicoutimi, Quebec. I was distracted and slammed my thumb in the car door as it shut. My dad and brother forced the door open, and my smashed thumb just hung there. I was in shock as my dad wrapped a diaper around my thumb to stop the bleeding. As the throbbing pain set in, I was told to sit still and put pressure on the injury. My father rigged a popsicle stick with a butterfly bandage to create a temporary splint. Looking back on this painful memory, I am certain the calm my parents exuded was their attempt to not create more pain, but I felt as if I was a burden and my injury was an inconvenience for them. *Don't cry, don't carry on, just brush it off and keep going.* But it did get me out of doing the dishes for a few days.

Growing up a middle child in a military family in Canada was, despite my feelings of being ignored and occasionally inconvenient, an interesting and mostly happy life. Though my father was a disciplined man in his professional life, at home he was very funny, a man who loved to make us all laugh. He had a special love for his four daughters and all of us vied to be his favorite. I loved the nickname he gave me, Blackie, which made me feel special. I remember animated conversations around the dinner table where each of us talked about whatever was going on in our lives. It was the opposite of what my father experienced as a child growing up with an alcoholic father who was also addicted to gambling, a child who never knew what life would be like from one day to the next. Because of his own difficult and insecure childhood, my father was determined to give his own children the security and stability he never had. We were all so proud of him, a man who came from a family who struggled in many ways. He and his siblings became incredibly resilient and learned to use laughter to embrace life and diffuse the sorrowful times. These are the aunts and uncles I came to respect and adore as I was growing up. He never showed any of the pain he was feeling whether from financial worries or the terrible ulcers from which he suffered for decades. We never knew any of that but went camping and snowmobiling and traveled around Europe in a tent trailer he and my mother built together. In our inside lives, we learned good manners, how to clean a house, and how to behave wherever we were. We were respected in all of the communities where we lived, and my parents took pride in that. They taught us we would be seen as a reflection of them, and they wanted and needed that impression to be a positive one.

I looked for happiness and support wherever I could. A born extrovert, growing up on military bases was easy for me. I made friends quickly and took part in all the available activities and sports. Before I became too comfortable or was able to make deep connections with people, we would pack everything and move. A new military base, new friends, no real intimacy, no deep emotional experience.

From the age of nine, I became aware that men and older boys were drawn to me, and I felt empowered by the attention I received. It made me feel noticed and significant, especially to a 14-year-old neighborhood boy. One day I was visiting my girlfriend and walked by her brother's bedroom door. It was cracked open, and I looked inside. He was exposed and touching himself. He invited me in and asked me to touch him. My curiosity led me in, and I did as he asked. Only a few minutes passed before I heard my girlfriend holler for me, so I jumped up and walked out of his room. Though that moment was incredibly inappropriate, I felt no shame, but quite the opposite. I had someone's attention. Three years later, I was babysitting when the dad came home early, a little drunk. He began to compliment me while kissing and touching me, and once again I allowed it, feeling powerful because I could see how much I excited him. He knew it was wrong and stopped after a few minutes. Later, I understood that although these were not violent acts against me, they were the moments in my too-young life that I lost my innocence. They would flavor the way I saw myself and establish my belief that men could not be trusted.

I never saw my parents fight or get into any conflict that needed resolution. I had no clue what arguments looked like or that it was normal for couples to disagree. They never said one bad thing to or about one other. They only showed love and mostly physical love. I would learn at an early age that conflict signals the end of a relationship. We were never allowed to say words such as hate or call each other names.

The only feelings we were allowed to show were happy ones, just the good stuff. I came to fear and avoid confrontation of any kind. In my home, it was not okay to indulge in sadness or feel sorrow inside. I was never allowed to fail and experience either the pain of failure or the self-confidence in recovering from that failure. Without that knowledge, I became focused on my exterior self and became, in a very real sense, anesthetized inside. I would only find a sense of self-importance emanating from my physical appearance and what I could give to others. After failing to get the attention I needed from my parents from the wounds of my early childhood, I stopped seeking approval and affirmation at home.

I was 13 and my boyfriend was 15, beautiful, smart, and liked by everyone who knew him. I liked him too, a lot. We dated for the next six months and went to all of the teen activities and sports events on the base where we lived. I was starving for attention, and he gave me everything I needed and was not getting from anyone else. We played around sexually, but never had intercourse. He was the only person in my life who made me feel as if I mattered, that I belonged. Then he left me. He told me I was too intense for him, that my neediness overwhelmed him. Heartbroken and devastated, I once again felt insignificant.

My father saw me in tears one day and asked what was wrong. For one of the first times in my childhood I expressed my feelings. My father's first response was that he was amazed I would care that much about this boy. And then his predictable refrain: "You're going to be fine. Just shake it off, pick yourself up, and move on." It would take many years for me to process the other message my father was giving me... that I was strong, I could handle heartbreak, and everything would, in time, be okay. His words toughened me inside and helped create a protective shield that kept me safe from being wounded by love again. It was necessary armor, and I would need it in my future, but that shield was not entirely impenetrable.

Our family was transferred again, this time to a military base in Goose Bay, Labrador, Canada. I graduated from high school at 15 and hung out with kids who were a couple years older. I felt mature, but of course I was not.

A few years after healing from my agonizing breakup with my boyfriend, my heart was crushed again, this time by my father. He was engaged in a lively conversation with a couple of his friends when I went to join them and share my opinions. My father looked at me and said in full view of his friends: "LouLou, you don't know what you're talking about. This conversation is way over your head." I walked out of the room in shame, embarrassed, devastated, and feeling completely unimportant. My intellectual," inside-self" felt dead, of no value to anyone. My relationship with my father, once strong and loving, had fractured. I doubt he knew how much his words hurt me. I was no longer his "favorite" and within a year, at the age of 17 I moved away from home. It took courage to take this step at such a young age, but the independence I developed as a child gave me the strength and belief in myself that I could do anything. My parents were right. I could pick myself up and move on.

I moved into a cute little apartment close to the University of Ottawa where I worked in the Career Counseling Center and began studying psychology, to learn more about others and myself. My apartment was right above a Chinese restaurant, and I loved decorating it and setting up my own home. On the same day I moved in, the man who would become my first husband moved in with me. I met Gary at a club on the military base, and was drawn to his sense of humor, his sexiness, and the fact that many women looked at him and wanted to be his partner. Though he looked fine on the outside, inside he was depressed and going through a very rough spell, just coming out of a painful relationship. Still, I was drawn to him because I thought he needed me, and I desperately wanted someone to need me. I assumed what many women assume, that I could fix him. Being with Gary would give my life purpose and some direction. We had some great times together playing cards with my sister Denise and her husband Joe and going dancing. Gary was an amazing dancer and we really connected in that way.

Within six months, I was pregnant, miserable, and not feeling any love or support from Gary or my parents to keep the child. I felt abandoned, alone, and insignificant and though I wanted a baby, I could not keep it. After my abortion in NYC – it was still illegal in Canada – I felt figuratively and literally empty and devastated. Whatever self-worth remained, evaporated. I was depressed, felt ugly, and hated myself, caring so little about what happened to me that I became pregnant again within six weeks. This time, my father somehow arranged for the abortion at the base where he was stationed. Two babies gone. My decision not to give birth to these children would haunt me for a very long time. Thirteen years later at 30 I joined Open Arms, an organization helping people traumatized by abortion who were looking for support. The group helped me to acknowledge my decision, eventually forgive myself and, as an act of love, give my unborn babies names: Rose and Hannah. This was my way to honor their existence and help me move forward.

I believed I was a terrible human being and began eating my way deeper into my misery. I was trying to fill an emptiness inside and I ate to keep people away. I was convinced no one could love me if I was fat. But no matter how much I ate, I never filled that deep void. I felt unworthy and gorged on junk food. I asked myself "who would want me" and made certain with every pound I gained, no one ever would. Gary said all the right words, that he loved me, and though I heard what he said, I was unable to receive them. I felt ugly, disgusting, and unworthy of love from anyone. Still, Gary asked me to marry him and believing that moment would be the only chance I would ever have to find anyone who wanted me, I said yes. I was 18 , 80 pounds heavier on the outside, and carrying around a much-bigger burden inside. I was adept at masking the interior pain I was carrying and fortifying the armor outside, but it was beginning to crack.

I sat in my bathtub one night, feeling more alone than ever, drank a bottle of wine, and let the pain and tears pour out. How had I arrived at this terribly sad place? Is this how I wanted my life to be? What could I do to change things? These questions haunted me as I allowed myself, for perhaps the first time in my life, to feel what I was feeling. I thought Gary deserved more and believed deeply I did as well.

I joined Weight Watchers, started an exercise class, and got a new job working at a foreign-exchange program for a government agency. I also began pushing Gary away as I continued to work on myself. My psychology classes helped me take a good, hard look inside myself. Gary was trying fiercely to hold me down and keep me where I was. We began fighting about every little thing, but at the heart of each argument was the fact that I was pulling away. Another terrible lesson from my childhood crept in; that couples are not supposed to fight or argue and if they did it meant the relationship was over. In my case that proved to be true. Against his wishes, Gary and I separated.

Over the next year and a half, now living alone in another small apartment, I lost 75 pounds and, ultimately, my first marriage. I began to imagine a better future for myself, which did not include Gary or anyone else in my life up to that moment. I needed to be free and come and go as I wished. I felt bold and confident that I would be fine. I asked, "what is the worst thing that could happen?" That I might fail? I could live with that. My motto became "if it feels good, do it."

I lived with few boundaries, unaccountable to anyone but myself. I explored my sexuality freely, which led to many relationships. But despite having many people around me, I felt empty and lonely and learned quickly this was not a path I wanted to walk. I searched for something to take me away from the life I was now living, something that would give my life purpose and I found it. I came upon a job opening as an administrative assistant to the president of a corporation in the Northwest Territories. A potential job 500 miles away geographically and far from the life I was living. I applied, was offered the position, but my father disapproved. Initially I turned-down the offer, but after struggling with the decision I called to see if the job was still available. It was. My military life and resounding message from my childhood that I could handle anything prepared me for this.

I welcomed the challenge of doing something others thought I should not or could not do. I was determined to cultivate a "can-do" spirit, which unbeknownst to me, was going to be a fundamental life skill that would help me face the unimaginable challenges to come. I packed my clothes and personal belongings and moved to the Great White North. I was going to live with the Inuits, far from all the places and people I knew. I was about to become a stranger in a strange land. At 22, I was young, thin, free, and emboldened.

CHAPTER 2

Fire and Ice

"Strong women aren't simply born. They are made by
the storms they walk thru."
—anonymous

On September 1, 1980, I landed in a tiny community that
rested on the western coast of Hudson Bay in the Northwest
Territories. It was the first snowstorm of the season and
looking out the window I saw a vast white landscape dotted
with a few, small buildings. The small plane skidded along a
hand-built runway and came to a stop in front of a single-wide
mobile home. This was the airport terminal. I immediately
wondered what I had gotten myself into and whether defying
my father's advice was a smart idea. My nomadic military life
had prepared me for change and taught me to adapt to new
surroundings, but this landscape was unlike anything I had
ever seen. I was hundreds of miles away from everything and
everyone I knew, but I was here and determined to succeed.

I was greeted outside by a statue of an Inukshuk, a
structure made of rough stones, six feet high, stacked in the
form of a human figure. These imposing creatures, I would
later learn, were strategically placed by the Inuit people as
landmarks, and used over thousands of years to help them
navigate as they hunted caribou, created new villages, and
lived their lives in a very challenging climate. It was not just

the landscape that was startling and so different. The language was truly foreign. Though I spoke both French and English, the Inuktitut dialect had a throaty, guttural sound and seemed strange, but intriguing. I could hardly speak it, let alone understand what was being said, though I was determined to learn it. At first these indigenous people seemed shy and distant, but within a few weeks I got to know some of the families and felt more relaxed, accepted, and embraced. My friends had often said that I "knew no strangers." I breathed easier and felt I belonged.

I settled into a tiny, three-room apartment, assigned to me by the company that hired me and which, thankfully, included a running toilet. I had the luxury of indoor flush toilets, electricity, and government-built homes with small office buildings scattered throughout the town. Many communities relied on honey buckets inside their meager homes, blocked off only by a small curtain. These portable buckets had bags inside and each night during the winter they were tossed out behind the houses to freeze. During the spring thaw, a truck would come around, pick up the still-frozen bags and dispose of them. I always wondered where they were dumped.   I was learning more than their language as I began to love the quiet of this new wilderness. I was learning a completely new way of life. I was cultivating bravery and building inner strength, believing that I could handle big changes. I was developing self-reliance and becoming compassionate towards people who were disadvantaged and in need.

I began my job as an administrative assistant to the president. My boss, Tulok, was 13 years my senior. He was a prominent politician within the community, handsome in a rugged way, and very intelligent. There were no movie theaters, bars, or restaurants in the small village and we would often go to my place or to his after work, to eat dinner and play cards. I soon discovered his interest in me was more than just professional and we became romantically involved.

Tulok made me feel significant and as if I belonged and mattered, something I always searched for and needed, especially in this new, strange place. Old patterns, however, started to return. I began partying and I fell back into a sense of self-doubt and shame. I had come here to reinvent myself and to try and be a different and better person. Once again, I found myself in a bathtub, drinking a bottle of wine, and losing hope for a better future. Tulok sensed my depression and invited me to visit his Pentecostal church. I turned down his offer, having grown up in a Catholic home with all the trappings I found fake, meaningless, and boring. The only part of church I ever enjoyed was watching my father sing and direct the choir. The rest of it felt hypocritical. I believed in God because I was told to, but had no idea who or what God was. I felt lost, empty, and guilty being in a personal relationship with my boss, but I finally agreed to go with him to this small, missionary church.

The preacher got my attention. I was struggling to be in control of my life, caught between my old life and this new way of living. I was reaching for a life raft and felt as if I could grab on to this preacher's words. He spoke of God in a deep and personal way and made me believe God loved me just as I was and wanted to lead me and guide me down a path where I could discover a sense of purpose and joy.

One day, alone in my tiny living room, drinking a glass of wine, I negotiated with God. I remember saying "If you can change me, make me a better person, and help me find inner peace and purpose, I will serve you." I ended with "I'll give you one year!" The audacity of giving God an ultimatum! I instantly felt a warmth flood over me, and a deep sense of peace came with it. I felt whole for the first time in my adult life.

Believing we often teach what we need to learn, I began teaching Sunday school to the young children in my village, teaching the Bible I had never bothered to study. God seemed to fill the dark, confused places of my soul and I felt a sense of rebirth. My intimate relationship with my boss continued and I struggled knowing it was against the teachings of the church.

When he asked me to marry him, I said yes and saw his proposal as a way to avoid burning in Hell and continuing to betray God. He was a persuasive man and gave me the validation I always craved. I was in awe of the fact that someone of his stature would want me and, once again, I felt special and significant. We continued working together, sleeping together, and planning a life of camping, hunting, and long trips in the frigid winters over the ice and snow. I was 23 and the possibilities seemed endless and exciting.

On one of our many trips over the frozen tundra to visit his family, I remember wearing a very heavy beaver coat, pants, and Kamiks – boots made of seal skin with a duffle lining. I was being pulled on a sled behind my fiancé driving a snowmobile. My eyes were covered by goggles and not an inch of skin was visible anywhere on my body. We were suddenly caught in a terrible blizzard, a complete whiteout and could not see even inches in front of us. But this was his comfort zone, he was the expert navigator and I trusted him. The temperature hovered somewhere around 50 degrees below zero with the wind rushing around us. He had made this trip hundreds of times and seemed to know where he was going, but as we passed a small stream, the sled tipped over and threw me into the icy water. Hypothermia set in quickly as he gathered me up, put me back on the sled, and covered me with caribou furs and seal skins. He drove as fast as he could to a nearby rustic home, inhabited by an Inuit family he knew. While my clothes were washed and dried, they fed us soup and sat us close to a fire. We continued our journey the next day and, for me, this would make a good story for my future children and grandchildren. I made light of the whole episode. Minimizing danger and uncomfortable experiences was becoming a way of life for me and would become a way to survive a future I could never have imagined.

As my fiancé and I traveled throughout the Northwest Territories, I saw both the beauty of its indigenous people and their pain. I met talented Inuit artists who created magnificent carvings of soapstone and narwhal tusks, beautiful prints and paintings. Their art came from their tribal pasts, but they were humans stuck between their native world and Western culture now infusing their lives. They had become dependent on our food, gas, vehicles, housing, and, inevitably, the alcohol and drugs were permeating many of their lives. I saw signs of terrible physical abuse, especially targeting women and young people. Though I had ignored the signs for many months, physical abuse was becoming part of my life as well.

For months, Tulok showed signs of uncontrolled rage that were intensifying. I made excuses for him and told myself it was okay for him to lash out. I believed, as I had in my first marriage, that I could fix him, and I was certain he would change for me. I was wrong.

On a clear afternoon, in the middle of winter at his home, we were talking about something I cannot remember. What I do recall is he got out of his chair, walked over to me, pushed me hard against the wall, and began screaming. The more I told him to stop, the angrier and more aggressive he became. He threw me to the floor, pushed me around and continued yelling at me. I cowered in a corner, covered my head, and begged him to stop as he continued pacing around the room, totally out of control. He punched a hole in the wall above where I was crouched, and I was terrified the next blow would hit me. I was desperately trying to find a way to escape his wrath. After an hour he finally calmed down and left, but the absolute terror of that moment instilled a fear in me I had never known. My first reaction, once things settled down, was that I must have done something to deserve this. I needed to be a better, more supportive partner. I believed what the church taught, that I needed to accept his repeated apologies and forgive him because that is what a good, Christian woman should do. I prayed. What I interpreted as the answer to my prayers came in the body of a woman named Susan who had set up small, mission churches throughout the Northwest Territories. She knew about Tulok's anger and abusiveness with his previous wife and girlfriends and offered me a way out of this crisis.

I moved again, this time to the Western Arctic thousands of miles away. I had nowhere else to go and, believing my life was in danger, I quietly planned my escape. I let the home office know that I was quitting my job and leaving. I got a friend to help me pack my furniture and clothes, and shipped everything to my sister's home in Calgary. Susan offered me a volunteer position to help her administer the bible college she had established then arranged for a small plane to fly me to the Western Arctic while my abusive fiancé was away on a hunting trip. I was terrified he would return before I left, but the moment the wheels left the ground I finally felt safe. Again, as with every move I had made in my life, I believed I was on my way to a better place.

My previous job had paid well and all living expenses had been covered so I knew that I could fully support myself with the savings I had set aside. The bible college had about 15 Inuit students and as I supported them, I, too, was learning about the God who had always been a stranger to me. I found peace in my life and a sense of belonging and purpose in helping others. I helped with the administration of the college as well as with cooking, cleaning, baking bread, and emptying the honey bucket every night.

Despite experiencing 24-hour darkness during the winter months, the quietness gave me a peaceful feeling. With no streetlights to block out the skies or dim the stars, I felt God's presence watching the vibrant colors of the Aurora Borealis... the Northern Lights. The blues and greens were mesmerizing, swaying back and forth, dancing for hours. The lights are caused by the interaction of the solar wind and the earth's magnetosphere. Though I had seen photos of this phenomenon, seeing it with my own eyes, so close I could almost touch it, made me believe God's hand was touching me. Feeling God's presence and relying on God's support began here and would be a sustaining force in my life. In those moments, I felt truly alive, but those feelings were fleeting. No one could have guessed inside I was still feeling disconnected, insignificant, and unworthy of love.

Although the blood and gravel of my childhood helped me to pick myself up and move on, it also left me with some deep scars. From a young age I learned to hide my pain and sadness behind exterior smiles. I still had a lingering feeling of being unworthy of love and care. I continued questioning whether I'd ever find a relationship where I felt truly seen and valued and safe from harm.

A few months after working in the glorious Western Arctic, I felt like I needed to establish more purpose and direction in my life. I decided to take a job volunteering as a counselor at a youth camp. I had never been to a summer camp and was excited about this adventure with this group of very lively young people. I was, in a sense, getting to be a bit of a kid again. As I was about to lift my suitcase onto the truck that would take all of us to Vancouver Island, a hand reached out to stop me. And there he was, dirty blond hair and incredibly handsome, with a crooked smile, asking me if I wanted to keep my guitar with me or put it in the back of the truck. Keith. Charming, cool, quirky Keith.

While at camp, we frequently bumped into each other and seemed to have the same duties at the same time and in the same places. We led daily Bible studies, supervised various camp activities, and he led worship at church services. We talked about the vision we had for our lives. I wanted to be a missionary in an underdeveloped country, and he wanted to be a pastor serving others. In a week, we formed a bond without ever holding hands. The night before camp ended, as he was about to leave for Seattle, he told me he wanted us to be together and asked me to pray about it.

For the next few weeks, after he had returned home and I was still at camp, we exchanged letters through fellow counselors. I returned to Vancouver 2 weeks later at the end of camp and Keith called me. We met a few days later and drove to Mt. Baker, a huge, active volcano, part of the Cascade mountain range east of Seattle. We sat under a tree by a stream and Keith, declaring his love for me, told me he believed we were meant to be married. I had been thinking of him and the life we could share and he seemed to fit the perfect picture I had of a husband. Keith seemed to have many of the things I thought I wanted in a man. He loved God, taught Bible college, was a musician, and was athletic. He was also charming and very handsome. I was a person who wanted to serve others and Keith seemed to want that too. It felt like a good match, and the answer to my quest for a partnership where I felt seen and valued, so I agreed to marry him. On August 29, 1982, my 25th birthday, I moved to Seattle and Keith and I announced our engagement.

It's funny how these momentous life choices play out in hindsight. I realize now, whatever it was that was propelling me toward this marriage had little to do with Keith and everything to do with becoming the best version of myself. I had no idea of the shattering trials ahead for us, nor of the immense gifts these trials would bring. I now believe it was much more than my fear and insecurity. It was me guiding myself to the incredible life lessons I was meant to live.

CHAPTER 3

Marriage and Motherhood

"Where you stumble, there your treasure lies. Only in
pain do we grow and become better."
—Joseph Campbell

From the beginning, life with Keith was difficult. Here we
were planning a wedding before we barely knew each other.
Keith complained about how unhappy he was that I was
divorced and how that might limit his ability to minister in
certain churches in the future. Some taught against remar-
riage, that it was a sin. I was determined to make this
relationship work, even though I was immediately starting to
have concerns.

We were married in our small, non-denominational
church in south Seattle. The only person who came, other than
church members and Keith's family, was my older sister
Denise who flew in from Calgary. Though I was nervous and
felt some uncertainty whether Keith would be able to accept
my past life, it was nevertheless a mostly happy occasion.
Keith was still critical of what he called my "poor decisions,"
but he would repeatedly tell me how much he loved me and
that God forgives us all.

Keith had a personal experience with God's forgiveness. A
star athlete in high school, he became addicted to illegal drugs.
He was a promising young "golden boy" with a possible future

as a professional baseball player or skier. One night he overdosed, put a sheet over his body and face and told God if he woke up the next morning, he would change his life and dedicate it to God's service. He did wake up and, after attending a Billy Graham crusade, gave his heart to Jesus. It was at that moment he felt called to be a pastor and bring God's word to others. At a young age he learned the hard way about the consequences of poor choices and forgiveness, but yet struggled forgiving others, including his new wife. It was disturbingly clear from the very first days after the wedding, we had very different ideas about marriage.

My parents' marriage was built on teamwork, children, and having fun. I never heard them argue or express any anger towards one another which, in hindsight, was not necessarily a good thing. I never learned how to resolve conflict because I never saw it happen and wrongly assumed if people fought it meant the death of a relationship. In time, I learned that was not true. Keith had grown up in a home completely different from my own, with conflict and fighting as the norm, not the exception.

From the outset, Keith and I argued a lot, far too much for what should have been the easiest and happiest times in a young marriage. I felt he was trying to control me and make me into the church's idea of the perfect Christian wife, and I was resisting. I understood how the church and my husband wanted me to be as a woman and wife, and I knew what I believed spiritually about these roles and my place. However I was learning to think more independently about who God was to me personally and had separated that from my relationship with the church. I didn't agree with some of the teachings of the church although fundamentally I had come to believe in God and His love for me. When we were with friends or family, Keith would criticize me publicly for laughing at an off-color joke or humiliate me by saying I was not being a good witness to others about the teachings of the church. Outside our home we put on a good show as a newly married, happy couple and I did not contradict him in public. No one would have ever guessed the constant turmoil going on when we were alone. In private, I would fight back and let him know he was not my God and I would not allow him to dictate my behavior. The conflict and turmoil were tumultuous and, as time went on, I felt that I was failing as the wife he needed me to be. The failed relationships of my past haunted me, and I questioned if I would ever get it right.

Despite the ugly and painful fights, we both wanted the marriage to succeed and sought counseling from our pastor. I was desperate to be the wife Keith wanted me to be, someone involved in the church ministry, someone who presented herself in a humble and modest way, even though I knew deep inside me that was not who I really was. It was truly who I wanted to be, but Keith's unrelenting pressure to turn me into the perfect Christian wife rankled me and went against my fiercely independent nature and deep need not to be controlled. For a while, the counseling helped. Our pastor encouraged me to be intentional and committed to honoring Keith, to basically "fake it" until I felt it. It worked for a while. I tried hard to keep my mouth shut and not to react to Keith's comments even when they deeply offended me. Keith tried to make some effort to understand my need for independence my resistance to conform merely because I was told to. He seemed to like my free-spirited ways, yet still struggled with them. I had friends, though, who revealed in that part of me, who loved that I sometimes colored outside the lines.

When I think back to what made it possible to face what I was about to endure and what would ultimately transform my life in such profoundly beautiful ways, I am certain none of it would have been possible without my friend network. In an odd way, I can see now that my struggles with Keith helped me strengthen and solidify the exact skills and priorities that would help me to thrive in the future. I learned at an early age the value of forming close friendships. Even though my military life moved me around every two years, I was always good at making new friends and found comfort, support, significance, and a sense of belonging in those connections. I believed then – and still do – that to have good friends I would have to be a good friend. I invested time and energy honing that skill from an early age and caring deeply for my friends, who were mostly girls. This was the beginning of forming my tribe, a group of girls and eventually women who, to this day, are deeply embedded in my life. These were, and are, my confidantes, the women who love and accept me for the true person I am. These are the people to whom I feel truly "married," the girls and women I would never and could never divorce, the women who would never leave me. Through life, death, failure, illness, bad hair days, diets, and wardrobe fails, we are truly together until death "do us part." My best kind of friendships have always been fierce and female, where we believe the best in each other and think each deserves the world.

It did not help my relationship with Keith when he lost his job as a building maintenance man after a few equipment accidents. He once rammed a forklift into the building and after two more incidents, he was fired. I could not work for six months after moving to Seattle because of immigration laws. With some experience painting houses and no heavy equip-ment needed, he took painting jobs in the area. I had some savings left from my time working in the Northwest Territor-ies, but it was not enough to support us for long.

After living a relatively comfortable life for most of my 25 years, I found myself standing in line at the food bank, trying to figure out how to make a chicken last for five meals. It was humbling, scary, and painful. I stood in line outside of the building with many others, mostly women, waiting my turn. On the outside I was well dressed and seemed confident, and could feel the harsh stares of others who seemed to judge me for even being in that line. I was completely humiliated at being unable to feed and provide for my family and I felt ashamed that I needed to rely on charity and the kindness of strangers to make ends meet. I had always been a strong and self-reliant woman and now I felt weak and humbled. Silent tears rolled down my cheeks and I wiped them away quickly, determined to do whatever it took to help my family. There were others in that line who looked at me with compassion and understanding. I would always remember their kindness and vowed to pay it forward someday. The reality was I was judging myself and feeling guilty. In later years, this experience would make me more compassionate and less judgmental of others' suffering.   This would not be the last time in my life I would rely on help from others.

Within a couple of months, Keith found a job in the maintenance department of a health care facility and decided to go back to school to become certified as a heating and air-conditioning technician. Though he was prone to breaking things, his charm and eagerness drew people to him and he found work despite his clumsiness. I was finally able to take a job as an accountant with a small company. Together, we crawled out of our financial mess and after a couple of years we decided to paint houses together and scraped up enough money for a down payment on a small home. I moved on to a new job in human resources at Seattle's Westin hotel and Keith continued working at the health care facility. We had some good times and enjoyed activities such as camping, skiing, and social events with friends from our church. Both of us were helping with the youth group at our church and Keith continued studying and teaching Bible classes. We were building a home, working full time, and trying to sustain a good marriage. With these common goals, the fighting and tension eased. These were happier times for us. We were a team, filling our home with love and, hopefully soon, with children.

At the age of 28, I was thrilled to discover that I had missed my period. I wanted to create a fun surprise for Keith announcing our pregnancy and set up the ultrasound appointment. My joy was short-lived when I saw the concerned look on the doctor's face after the exam. It was a tubal pregnancy with the egg lodged in the Fallopian tube and the pregnancy had to be terminated. The losses from my past two abortions haunted me and I wondered if I was being punished. My plan to surprise Keith with the wonderful news turned into deep sorrow for both of us, but we were young and felt confident we would eventually have children. I managed to stuff the pain of all my losses in some corner of my mind and kept as busy as I could at work and church so I would not have to think about the pain. By now I was becoming quite expert at burying my feelings.

Fortunately it didn't take long for me to get pregnant again and one year later Joshua James Chalcraft came into the world, an upside-down breech baby. While I was in labor, as I was feeling another contraction, Keith held up his hand and told me to wait a second, the Seahawks were about to score a touchdown. My excitement about the birth of our child overshadowed the shock of Keith's request. We laughed about it later, but I found his request disturbing. I could not have cared less whether the Seahawks scored. All that mattered to me was Joshua. He arrived calm and seemed ready to face the world. Having lost three children, I was filled with hope as I looked at my tiny boy. I remember praying he would be strong and healthy and have a positive impact in making the world a better place. The prayer that came into my heart was from Jeremiah 29:11:

> *"For I know the plans I have for you, says the Lord. They are plans for good and not for disaster, to give you a future and a hope."*

I believed that was what God had in store for my Joshua the day he was born. In the future, I would learn to redefine my expectations about what "good" and "hopeful" would eventually mean to us.

Joshua was an easy baby who came out of the womb smiling and never really stopped. Everywhere we went strangers would admire him and say what a beautiful baby he was. He rarely fussed and brought tremendous joy and laughter into our home. We thought we had the whole parenting thing figured out because he was so calm and easy to manage. From the beginning he was on a schedule for eating, sleeping, and even pooping, and rarely strayed from it. I quit working at the Westin and started a part-time, home-based business with a direct-sales company selling Christmas decorations. I wanted to stay home with my baby but needed additional income to help support our little family. Joshua was our joy and Keith and I were getting along better than ever before. We had a shared purpose in raising a healthy and happy child.

Six months later, I was pregnant again and lost this baby because of another tubal pregnancy. While that loss was horrible enough, my doctor's partner informed us he had to remove the one remaining fallopian tube, which meant we were not going to be able to have more children. Again, I believed God was punishing me for terminating my earlier pregnancies. I wept, mourning all the children I had lost, both from my physical problems and from my own painful choices. Two months later, in a follow-up visit to my obstetrician, I told him how sad I was about not being able to have more children. He looked at me, puzzled by what I said, and asked me why I thought that. He checked my file and said there was an error in the information that I was told. During the procedure they were actually able to preserve the tube which would allow the possibility of future pregnancies. I was elated.

Within six months, I was pregnant again and Leah Ann

Chalcraft came screaming into the world on April 10, 1987. Leah was the complete opposite of her brother Joshua. As he was calm and cheerful, she was a fireball, demanding and uncomfortable around a lot of noise and activity. She was strong-willed and determined to get her way, traits that would serve her well in the future. Completely bald until she was two, I put dabs of toothpaste on her little, shiny head and stuck on small bows to hide the fact that she had no hair. When she was 11 days old, in the French tradition, I had her ears pierced with tiny pearl earrings to prove she was a little girl. People still asked if she was a boy or a girl. Either way she was adorable. Cute, but feisty. My pride in being the perfect parent evaporated with Leah's birth. Unlike Joshua, who easily adapted to everything and was always happy, baby Leah wanted nothing to do with schedules for feeding or sleeping or really anything. Two humans from the same parents were unimaginably different.

Despite my exhaustion from living with two toddlers, I got pregnant again with my third tubal pregnancy. My doctor informed us that he was not able to preserve the one remaining tube and this ended the possibility of ever having more children. Over a period of three years, I had five pregnancies, a successful home business, and my continuing work at the church. As if that was not enough to handle, I

began babysitting a friend's two young sons, Alex and Andrew, as well as cleaning her house. We needed the money to help support our family. I thought I was indefatigable, that I could do anything, but I was pushing myself too far and too fast.

Keith was busy and distracted, focused on his job and

the church, and seemed not to notice what was happening to me. I resented the time he spent in his office, studying the Bible while I was left taking care of the house, the children, and trying to keep my own business running. He would come home from work, spend a few minutes with the babies, then disappear into his study until dinner time, a meal I felt responsible for cooking. When I would make occasional plans to spend an evening away with my girlfriends, he resented it and used guilt to try and prevent me from going out. He wanted me to stay home. I knew I needed to self-care and take time away from Joshua and Leah and my duties as a wife. I could feel a little resentment growing in my heart from feeling overwhelmed with responsibilities without any respite or relief. Even knowing that it would cause tension in our marriage, I went ahead and made the plans to get away. This was the beginning of forming an essential survival skill that would save me in so many ways as I walked through the many challenges to come. So many mothers are conditioned to sacrifice themselves for mothering and to want time away and to prioritize self-care is a sin and brings on guilt. If you are the parent of a child with disabilities or caring for an aging parent this can be magnified by a million.

One very fortuitous night, I went out with a girlfriend to a Pampered Chef party she was hosting. It was a new company in the direct sales Industry, a modern version of the popular Tupperware parties in the 1950's and 1960's. Consultants held home parties, where they cooked a recipe to demonstrate and sell their first-rate kitchen tools. The consultant on that night picked up on my extroverted personality and enthusiasm for her products. After I jumped at the chance to help her demonstrate a tool and entertain the guests, I was hooked. I loved people, loved being the focus of their attention, and loved making them laugh. Here was a new door opening. I walked through it without hesitation and began a journey that continues to the present day, a decision that helped other women succeed in their lives and sustained me in the trials that lay ahead.

My new venture gave me an identity other than being a wife and mother and would, in the decades ahead, help distract and save me from a daunting, unimaginable, and frightening future. I felt empowered and in control of this one area in my life and it became the reason and excuse I needed to "get away" when attending conferences and incentive trips. It also gave me financial freedom which allowed me to provide many things for my family. After a few months, I left my accounting job and began my Pampered Chef business. It was a perfect fit for me. Within six months, I reached the level of director and over the years promoted to executive director, achieved by hiring and training other women to become consultants. While Keith was happy with the extra income I was earning, he was not pleased my job meant occasional weeknights and weekends away from him and the children.

The terrible fighting that had plagued our early marriage began erupting again. The same pattern of someone trying to control me and my ensuing resentment was repeating itself. I felt almost invisible and insignificant to Keith and angry he could not see what I was going through and how exhausted I was from taking on far too much responsibility at home and in helping provide for our family. When we found time to talk, he told me I was not meeting his expectations as a wife and failing to support him in his goals to become a pastor, but I had nothing left to give. His expectations did not align with who I was or how I wanted to fulfil these roles and was conflicted. I felt guilty, weak, but also angry about what was happening in my life and my marriage of only seven years. I later realized that it was these exact tendencies—to prioritize fulfilling my life over fulfilling his that made it possible for me to be a strong mother and caregiver for my children. I was learning to fight for the skills and priorities that would ultimately save me.

We went to couples counseling once again. Though I had almost no physical or emotional attraction to Keith, I was still determined not to let this marriage fail, if only for the sake of our young children. These struggles were real, devastating, and painful because I somehow knew our marriage would, in the end, not survive.

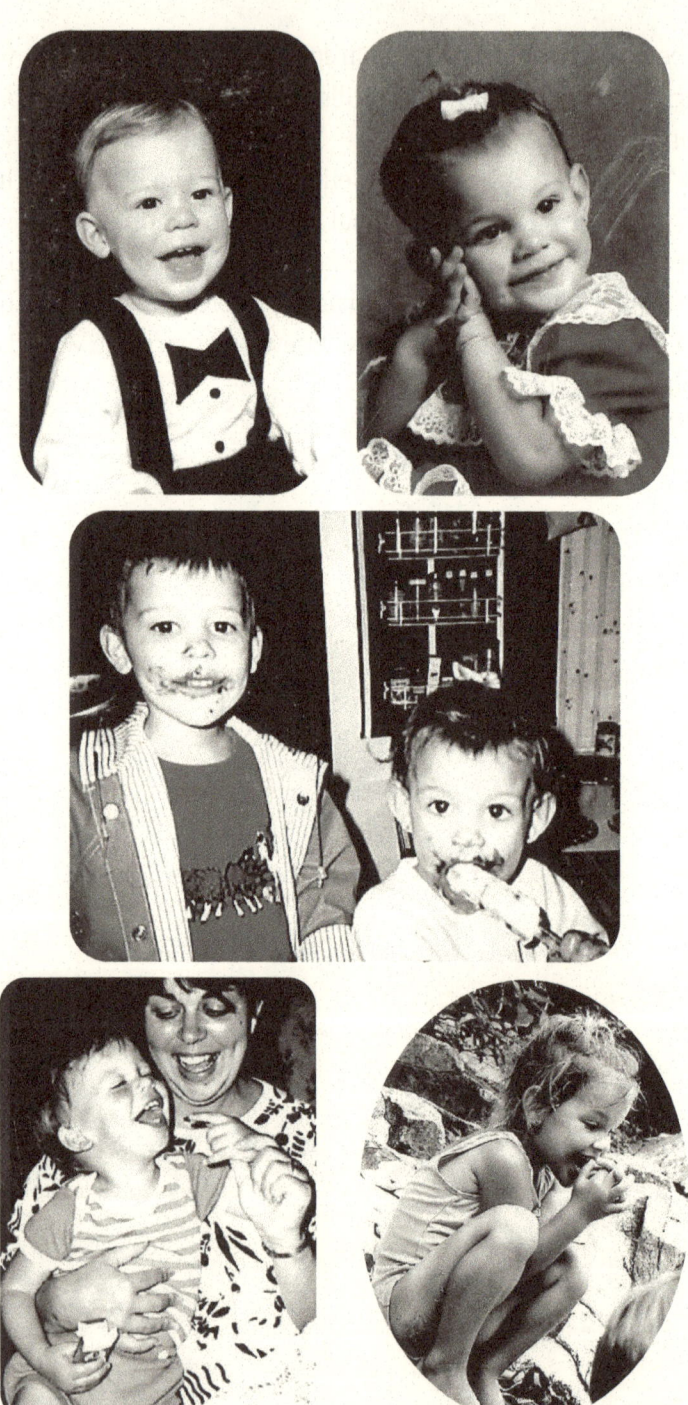

PART TWO

CHAPTER 4

Into the Darkness

"Everything you love will probably be lost, but in the end, love will return in another way."
—Franz Kafka

Anyone who has been faced with learning that something is terribly wrong remembers that moment in great detail. It's the moment when all the questions, asked and unasked, are answered and our worst fears can no longer be denied. All hope of a different outcome is lost and we are forced to face the hard, incomprehensible truth. Life as we know it will never be the same.

At Joshua's third birthday party, watching him run and play with other children, I noticed how tired he looked, with dark circles under his eyes and saw he often had to stop, sit down, and rest. It was not the first time I noticed his fatigue but here, comparing him to his buddies abilities, it was more obvious. Over the previous 6 months, my friends had made slight mention of their concern but I had brushed it off. I was aware but thought if I don't say it out loud, it won't be true. The other kids did not seem to struggle this way. He kept tripping over small things, losing his coordination, stumbling and often losing his balance. None of his little friends exhibited any of these problems. He complained during the day of fatigue, of aching joints and muscles, and often woke up screaming in the middle of the night with pain in his legs and cramps rippling through his little body. I vividly remember picking him up gently from his bed, putting him in a hot bath, and massaging his legs for hours until his cramps and pain subsided. Keith and I were not the only ones who noticed something was terribly wrong. His preschool teacher, as well as some of our family and friends, noticed he often walked with a stagger and his gait seemed different and awkward compared with other children his age. Though he continued to take part in normal activities for his age group, Joshua often seemed content to sit on the sidelines, watching and cheering on his young friends.

Ever the optimist, I told myself these peculiar symptoms would pass, he would be fine, and this ordeal would eventually end. I took him to his pediatrician, a doctor experienced in working with special-needs kids. He first suggested possible growing pains as the cause of Joshua's problems, but said he seemed a bit young for that. He thought allergies might be a possible cause and asked us to take Joshua off dairy products to see if that might help. It did not. I kept watching, but the cramps and pain throughout his body did not go away and he struggled to breathe, which caused his fatigue.

I felt helpless and frantic that there was something quite serious happening, but with my habit of minimizing trauma to cope, I told myself it could not possibly be anything truly consequential. These symptoms continued for almost a year with neither relief nor respite for our baby boy or for us.

Finally, when Joshua turned four and with no signs of improvement and only indications things were getting worse, his pediatrician referred us to Dr. Steven Glass, a well known neurologist in Seattle. Dr. Glass did some preliminary tests and sent us to Seattle Children's Hospital to begin more diagnostic testing. I could no longer tell myself this was all going to magically disappear. Something was terribly wrong with Joshua and we had to find out what was happening and why. I am by nature a troubleshooter and a fixer and I just wanted to be able to fix this. So I kept pressing the doctors, becoming a persistent and often aggressive advocate for my son.

Keith continued to work and was not very involved in this process partly because I continued to minimize what was going on. I kept my emotions, fears, and concerns from him. He had a tendency to overreact and I just could not handle his emotional state. In retrospect, I told myself I was protecting him, but in fact I was protecting myself and our children from his despair. I had my little boy and Leah to care for and required all my focus, time, and energy.

Joshua was subjected to some very painful testing, which would have been terrifying to anyone of any age, but particularly frightening to a young child. As his mother, I would have traded places with him if that had been possible because watching him suffer through this ordeal was horrifying. I remember having to position my upper body on top of him to keep him motionless as the doctors conducted multiple tests of his nerve endings. Joshua said he was really afraid during these invasive tests and I told him I was afraid too. I said we would both have to be brave. We had to let the doctors do whatever they needed to do. I told him that is what it means to be brave, that it was okay to be afraid, but we still needed to push forward. I assured him I would never, ever leave him alone. We would do this together. He was comforted by my words and from that point on, I always praised him for being the bravest boy I knew. I'm not sure where these words came from other than my fierce need to comfort and protect my scared little boy. I imagine God had a hand on my heart and was guiding and directing my thoughts, even when I wasn't aware.

Keith was not with me during Joshua's tests and that is how I wanted it. I knew I was strong enough to handle things myself. In hindsight I may have been unfair to Keith, but that is how I felt at the time. I was in survival mode and did not trust or believe I could depend on him for emotional support. We struggled through two more years of diagnostic testing, searching for answers, but after all that time, there was none. There were no answers to be found in Seattle at that time. The doctors in Seattle sent us to the Oregon State Medical Center for more testing and more suffering for my Joshua. One of the first things the doctors did after they sedated him was to make a three-inch long incision into Joshua's thigh to extract a large tissue sample of muscle. They were trying to determine if he had a mitochondrial disease, which would explain the extreme fatigue he was experiencing. The mitochondria are the power pack in our cells and could explain his fatigue and shortness of breath.

They discovered this was not the problem and sent us back to Seattle Children's Hospital for additional neurological testing. As they searched for some medical explanation of what was causing his suffering, Joshua went through dozens of additional diagnostic exams, testing his gross and fine motor skills, gait, and balance. They tested his reflexes and administered vision and hearing tests. The doctors seemed to be getting closer to an answer, but required one final test to confirm their suspicions, the heart muscle biopsy, to determine whether he had hypertrophic cardiomyopathy, a thickening of the left ventricle of the heart. It seemed they were as confused about the symptoms as we were but did not want to alarm us with possibilities and guesswork without clear answers.

Every inch of his little body, inside and out, had been poked, invaded, and analyzed. Finally, after two and a half years of rigorous, invasive, and sometimes painful testing, the neurologist's receptionist called to set up an appointment with Dr. Glass to discuss the various test results in person. I walked into his office alone. I told Keith not to take time off from work and I would share the information with him when I got home.

I entered the doctor's office with a smile on my face, thinking again he had come up with a simple solution. I could not begin to imagine anything truly horrible could come from all the tests. I continued to live in a naïve bubble of optimism and denial, choosing to believe things would be fine. I was unprepared to hear the results.

Dr. Glass had put the pieces of the mysterious medical puzzle together. Joshua James Chalcraft, now six and a half, had no reflexes, poor balance, and coordination, delayed hearing, unusually high arches in his feet, nystagmus in his eyes causing them to move involuntarily side-to-side, and hypertrophic cardiomyopathy—to name just a few of his afflictions. My beautiful, strong, ever-cheerful young son was diagnosed with Friedreich's Ataxia, an extremely rare, genetic, neurological disease that affects all muscles in the body. It mimics ALS, or Lou Gehrig's disease, but its progression is much slower in children. While it typically appears in puberty, Joshua had started showing symptoms at the age of three. Only 20-thousand children at that time had been diagnosed. It was a disease with no cure. It was terminal.

The research was scant back in the early 90s though more than 150 years had passed since the disease was described by a German pathologist, Nikolaus Friedreich. In 1863, he described a new spinal disease which, more than a decade later, was attributed to a genetic defect as the cause. Unbeknownst to us, both Keith and I carried the recessive gene for FA. There is a 1 in 100,000 chance of having a partner carrying the same recessive gene and even with that statistic, there is only a 25-percent chance of having a child with FA. The research was terribly limited, and our physicians knew very little at the time.

Joshua had between five and 15 years to live and would soon end up in a wheelchair. He also had a 50-percent chance of losing his vision and hearing, possibly getting diabetes and would inevitably lose his balance and coordination. There was only bad and frightening news in the doctor's words, not even a little bit of hope. Joshua would likely require full spinal fusion surgery with a rod placed in his back due to scoliosis and need foot surgery if he wanted to continue wearing regular shoes. As horrific as those words were, they were just some of the predicted complications from the diagnosis of Friedreich's Ataxia. To make things even more hopeless, I was told there was nothing to be done. All we could do was to deal with each terrible symptom as it presented itself. The only glimmer of hope the doctor gave me was a referral to a national support group called the National Ataxia Foundation. He also mentioned that the Muscular Dystrophy Association was involved in the small amount of research being conducted for this incredibly rare disease. That was the last I saw of him. There was little else he could do.

I was in shock. I was numb. Nothing could ever prepare a parent or any human being to hear such horrific words. I have no memory of how I got home that day. I could not feel anything. I do remember thinking that God had betrayed me. After years of watching my son suffer, we finally had answers, but knowing those answers gave us little comfort. We finally had a diagnosis. We knew what it was, but the facts were unimaginably devastating and overwhelming. How could I trust in a God that would allow my child such pain and deny him a healthy life and future? The foundation of my faith, a God who loved us and wanted the best for us always, was shaken to the core. How could this possibly be the best for my beautiful son Joshua?

I somehow found my way home and had to tell Keith the news. I looked at him, my eyes filled with tears and with an incredibly heavy heart told him what the neurologist told me. It was impossible to digest this information all at once. This was unimaginable in so many ways. We sat there holding each other and sobbed for our little boy. Joshua and Leah were upstairs playing when I shared the news with Keith, but soon they came downstairs wondering what was going on. I remember that we hugged them, trying not to scare them, but needing to feel their warmth and wanting them to feel our love and protection. If we held them long and hard enough maybe this reality would go away. Maybe the diagnosis was wrong. Maybe a cure would be found in the very near future. We had no idea what that future would hold and for the first time since this nightmare began, I felt hopeless and utterly powerless. This was not something I or anyone else could fix.

The next couple of weeks were a blur as we tried to make sense of all we had been told. Keith dug into research on the disease, but there was little information to be found. I just held on to both of my children, trying to keep them safe and life as normal as possible. I focused mostly on their emotional state and realized if I showed any fear it might have a terrible impact on them. I went on autopilot just to get to the next moment, and the next, and the next. In some ways there was relief after years of testing and not knowing what was happening. We finally had a diagnosis and the answers we needed, but the truth was heartbreaking. In true form, Keith spiraled into depression with this news. He told me that he was supposed to protect and provide for his family and felt powerless and withdrew. He believed that his faith must not be strong enough to heal our child. Some church doctrines taught that and it seemed to stick in his mind. I never believed that for a minute. I knew that I could not control God by any means and for a reason I could never understand, He was allowing this. I do not believe He wants ill for us but I do believe that as our creator, He loves us and clung to that belief. I was determined to move forward, one way or another. My mother had taught me to brush it off and just keep going. Everything would be okay. By the age of 35 I had become an expert at not feeling pain or sorrow too deeply, though this was unlike any pain I could ever have imagined.

We had to tell Joshua. How do you tell a six-year-old such

a terrible truth? How can such a young child even begin to understand life and death or the gravity of his future? Keith and I discussed how to share this with Joshua and decided it was best to focus on encouraging him to dream big and allow him to live his life as normally as possible for as long as possible. I believed he would ask for answers when he was ready to hear them.

One bright and sunny spring morning we invited him out onto the side yard with us and sat on the swings Keith had built. He loved to be pushed high and always asked to go higher. After a few pushes we said we had something important to share with him. We told him his muscles were having a difficult time growing properly and that was why he felt tired a lot. With my heart full of desperate hope for healing from either God or a cure, we told Joshua that he would need to take medicine for his pain and it would help him feel better. He was given a beta-blocker to help with his heart muscle fatigue and a muscle relaxant to help with leg cramps. Both proved to be very effective as we moved forward into our unpredictable future. At his young age, he simply said ok and was ready to play some more. I knew more questions would come some day when he was ready and wanting to know more but for this moment, I was grateful for the gift of time. Perhaps it was because I did not want to believe the prognosis of a five to 15-year life expectancy for my son, or perhaps it was all the years of experience in brushing it off and moving forward, I convinced myself everything would be okay. I did not have the luxury of wasting time and did not feel I had the right to feel a despair that could have paralyzed me.

This was my truth. I had two children who needed their mother and at that time knew that my attitude and perspective would have a huge influence on how they would see themselves and their lives. Keith struggled with his depression, but his love for his children gave him strength to move forward as well.

Joshua's love of sports gave us a way to go into the future.

His hero was Ken Griffey Jr. and he was determined to be a baseball player just like him. He loved Michael Jordan and watched every basketball game, sure that he too could become a famous basketball player. From the age of three we had taken him on the slopes of Snoqualmie Pass and taught him how to ski. He loved it and although his balance was a challenge, Keith would put him between his own skis and glide down the snow-covered bunny hills, teaching his son to love a sport that he loved. We would take turns carrying two-year-old Leah in a backpack as Joshua practiced his moves. We soon determined this disease would not steal our son's love of sports. Joshua continued to find great joy in all his sports activities, especially skiing on the slopes with his dad. I can still hear his laughter as he would lose his balance and fall into the soft, fluffy snow on his way down the hill. He was known for his persistence and never giving up. He had earned awards at school in his early years, and this attitude would carry him well for the rest of his life. Every time he fell down he would simply brush it off, get up, and keep trying. Apparently, Josh had learned the lessons I was taught when I was his age. Had I modeled this to him from my own behavior, showing a positive spin on the challenges I was facing and never giving up? I knew this was an important skill he would need moving forward and encouraged him to take pride in doing his best at whatever he set his mind to. I assured him that his best was enough and that I was so proud of him. This helped him build confidence in his ability to survive and strive.

In our quiet time when we were alone, we continued to be haunted by a deep, dark sadness, but also felt compelled to move forward and make life as normal and upbeat as possible. This disease could shorten my son's life but I was determined it would not take away his joy or mine. In my own life, whenever I found myself in difficult situations and felt I could not trust or count on anyone, I often got stronger. I had learned self-care and to walk away from toxic situations. I found my way through difficult decisions that had to be made in relationships and I believed that same sense of strength would carry me through again.

When Keith and I told our friends in the church, they would, with the best of intentions, talk in cliches: *"God doesn't give us more than we can handle."* I remember thinking *"I wish God didn't have such confidence in me."* I hated all of the common sayings and quotes, but found grace for friends speaking those words to me. I knew I had likely said those same things many times to others facing difficulties.

I wondered though, as the words fell on my deaf and resentful ears, had anyone ever faced anything quite this terrible, to be told your young child faced a life of horrific challenges with no hope of recovery and only the prospect of dying young? Many of our friends did not know what to say and avoided us completely, which only added to our suffering. In time, though, I realized people just did not know what to say to comfort us.

I am not sure how I knew this, but intuitively I realized we would have to move toward our community and help them understand and support us if we were going to get through this all together. Understanding this helped me through this time as well as the years to come. I asked our pastor if we could share some thoughts at our church, without the children present. Keith and I stood in front of the congregation and explained Joshua's diagnosis of Friedreich's Ataxia. We shared what the doctors had told us about Joshua's prognosis. We told them that although we appreciated their desire to help, we had no idea what that help might look like. We just did not know. We only knew we were in shock and in terms of anything specific, we just did not know what we needed. We asked our friends to stop avoiding us just because they could not find the right words. There were no right words. We only asked that they sit with us from time to time in our darkness.

Some gestures were perfect, such as an anonymous gift I

got in the mail. It was a small bulb that I needed to plant, place on my windowsill, and continue to nurture. As I watched it grow into a beautiful lily, this new life felt like hope to me. My friend Janet knew I had always wanted to sew my own Christmas dress and took me to a fabric store to pick out supplies so she could help me. Having something to do with a beginning and an end was therapeutic and helped me begin to slowly crawl out of the dangerous and scary rut that threatened to swallow me. I had always loved tackling a project from start to finish. Just digging a hole for a plant and finishing a dress was helping me to breathe again. Still, after Joshua's diagnosis, I continued to struggle trying to concentrate on anything and felt a deep sadness still hovering over me. I could not have survived this moment of my life without my tribe of women. They carried me through by bringing meals, planning activities, arranging playdates with my children, and sometimes just sitting with me in moments of profound silence.

Though much of our focus and attention was on Joshua, Leah continued to be her normal gregarious self, running everywhere and being the drama queen in our home. When Joshua went for dozens of tests, Leah spent time playing at her friends' homes. She was still a toddler, only two-and-a-half when all of this began and, thankfully, seemed unaware of what was happening in our family.

Though Leah seemed unaffected by Joshua's situation, I began noticing she was walking more and more on her tiptoes. She would trip and fall easily, and we believed she was simply mimicking her brother to get our attention. She was stubborn, fussy, and irritated by a lot of noise and activity. I characterized her as an introvert, quite the opposite of her brother. She hated the big birthday parties I organized for her. I was trying to lavish attention on her, but these celebrations only made her miserable.

It was a month after the diagnosis, and I still had not told my parents the truth about Joshua. I was afraid they would minimize the reality of his dire prognosis and not give me the comfort I so desperately wanted and needed. I remembered too many times in my childhood when I was hurting – either from a fall on a bike, a break-up with a boyfriend, or their failure to support other successes –they failed to recognize my pain and give me the love I needed. They had always minimized what was happening and told me I was strong and could handle anything.

They reacted to the news of Joshua's diagnosis exactly as I thought they would. They diminished what I was telling them and echoed their words from my childhood. I was strong, I could handle this, everything would be okay. They gave me no comfort or emotional support. It was all I could do not to slam down the phone. I was not strong, and I did not want to handle any of this. I hung up after that empty conversation, wishing they had just been able to cry with me. Perhaps they cried on their own, but never in front of me. I did not cry either. I needed to. I wanted to, but did not give myself permission to release the agony I was feeling.

Keith was in his own dark place and retreated to his office to try and avoid our new reality. Our marriage was unraveling even before Joshua's diagnosis and now we were becoming even more distant from one another. We needed each other but were incapable of giving anything in the wake of our child's crisis. I kept my tears and pain at bay from my children as well. I did not want my six-year-old son and five-year-old daughter to sense my pain or my fear. I needed to remain strong. I wanted my sweet, innocent children to feel as normal and carefree as possible and any visible signs of dread or worry might have betrayed my responsibilities as their mother.

A week after Joshua's diagnosis, friends invited us to a movie they thought would be helpful. It had just come out and it made them think of us. Their intentions were good. The movie was called *"Lorenzo's Oil,"* about parents facing the diagnosis of their young son's terminal illness. After the movie we got into the car and sobbed. We were not ready to face the truth of our future. Our friends could not have known how we were just trying to hold ourselves together by a thread and how this movie took us deeper into our despair as we watched this family struggle on screen. It was, however, very therapeutic for Keith and me, in the quiet of our car and away from the children, to finally allow ourselves to grieve together. It was one of the few times I allowed myself to feel the deep and unrelenting sadness and pain for our family. Though I would come to learn how important this is for caregivers to do, for any of us really, it was hard for me and would remain hard. I came to learn it as a skill I had to cultivate, not a weakness I had to avoid.

As I worried about the future and how Joshua would navigate life in a wheelchair and live with the limitations he would face, a wise friend shared a life-changing thought with me. She said, "Louise, don't look at tomorrow and the challenges you will have to face in the future; you don't have to be ready for that right now. Just deal with the issues you have to face today. With time you will have the courage and strength to deal with tomorrow when it comes. Just take one day at a time." Those words echoed in my mind many times over the years and helped me when anxiety and fear overwhelmed me.

As Joshua continued to play t-ball and struggled to wobble around the bases, Keith would say to me how sad it was he could not run like the other boys. Keith had such a passion and talent for sports and was now incredibly heartbroken he could not dream about playing sports with his son. He focused more on what he was going to miss and less on what Joshua would miss. I tried to look on the bright side and would reply how wonderful it was that he was still loving the game and could still participate in every way. This became a source of contention between us and pulled us even farther apart. I resented his negative attitude and overcompensated with my positive one. He resented my optimism and once accused me of not caring at all about our son and the challenges he was facing because I never wanted to talk about them. I stood in front of him as he said that and hated him for not understanding that I chose not to live in a world without hope for my son. I needed to believe in a bright future and at least try to focus on better days ahead.

In hindsight, I now see that we were both processing our pain in opposite ways and needed someone outside of our relationship to help us find ways to understand and support each other. We were so deep in the weeds of our own emotions and I wish that someone would have suggested that to us. In all fairness, perhaps someone did and we just couldn't hear it at that time.

I remember one game when Joshua hit the ball and was barely able to wobble to first base. Our best friend, Uncle Alfie, came running over, scooped him up, and ran the bases with Joshua in his arms. The crowd cheered and Joshua held himself proudly as if he had just hit a home run! At that moment I knew my son would be okay. He had people who loved him. He was a bright and shining star among his peers, and his passion and joy of life would endear him to all who knew him for whatever years remained.

There were moments, though, when we were reminded of the profoundly sad truth of our present and our future. Joshua and his best buddy Jacob were in the back seat of our car, chatting, when Joshua called out to me and said, "Mom, Jacob said that I'm going to die." Jacob had overheard our dear friends, his parents, talking about Joshua and in his innocence shared what he had heard. For a moment, it took me off guard, but in a very calm voice I replied, "Joshua, we are all going to die and no one knows when that day or time will come. It's all up to God. We need to make sure that we are good people and

50

live every day the best we can, that's the most important thing." The boys seemed to accept my response as they continued to play and process my words as much as seven-year-olds could.

After Joshua's diagnosis, we contacted the National Ataxia Foundation to get some information on FA. They informed us there was an upcoming annual conference for families with all types of ataxias and invited us to go to Little Rock, Arkansas. We did not have the funds to pay for the trip, but an offering from the church allowed us to go to the conference. We were incredibly blessed by the love and support we received. It was another great decision, but also heart-breaking and difficult. We left Joshua and Leah with our dear friends, Uncle Alfie and Auntie Janet, and headed off to Arkansas. We met other parents of kids with Friedreich's Ataxia and in the breakout sessions learned from doctors and research scientists about the progress in finding a cure as well as experimental treatments and helpful ways of dealing with the physical and emotional aspects of FA.

It was painful to watch the older kids who were already in wheelchairs, but they did not look unhappy. They laughed, joked, teased, and enjoyed life just as other "normal" kids do and seemed so comfortable with their young friends. During one session where the kids spoke in their staggered slur, I listened as they shared what it was like to have FA and what they were doing to make the best of their challenging lives. They took part in the MDA telethons, the Firefighters' "Fill the Boot," and continued going to dances, proms, and school games. They encouraged each other with ideas about joining local wheelchair sports and yoga classes and a few even had a service dog.

All I could picture in the moment was my little boy in a wheelchair and I wanted to cry and continue denying what was going to happen to Joshua. The parents were very compassionate, remembering how it felt when their kids were first diagnosed. They sat with us in the darkness. At times we would go to our room and just cry. It was all too much to see and hear. The future looked bleak and ominous. How were we going to deal with this debilitating disease? We did not yet have those answers, but as we left the conference, we felt somewhat comforted and encouraged that life would go on and if others could do it, we could too.

We were now facing a different life than we had ever imagined or dreamed about, but we could still live a life filled with hope and dreams. I was intent on making each day meaningful and finding the gift in each moment. We had no time to waste. Whatever time remained mattered now more than ever. I was determined, with as much ferocity as I could muster, to shine some light into the darkness.

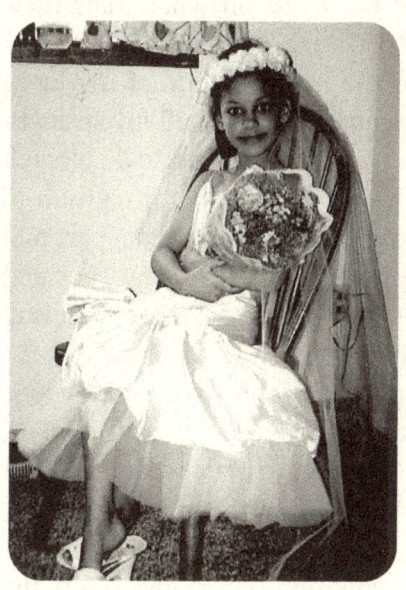

CHAPTER 5

A Wish Comes True

"Every day may not be GOOD... but there is GOOD in every day"
—anonymous

Shining light in the overwhelming darkness permeating our little family meant at every moment of every day I looked for things to be grateful for and happy about. I tried to see my children in the moment and not focus on what trials their futures may bring them. I tried to celebrate every success. Truth be told, it also helped me maintain one of my long-standing coping strategies—denial. Even with all my strength and determination this was not something I could do alone. I made a great effort to reach out to my tribe, my group of friends who I knew I could count on for the love, support and encouragement I needed to nurture and feed my soul and spirit. I was grateful that I had cultivated these beautiful relationships over previous years.

Keith's family and our generous church friends helped bring additional light into our lives. They gathered around us, trying and succeeding in finding ways to comfort and support us. They brought us meals when I was too exhausted mentally and physically to cook. They invited our kids to their homes for playdates with their own children to help give Keith and me some time alone to process what was happening to our family.

Love came to us in other ways as well and from strangers we had never met. People from the Make-a-Wish foundation called to tell us that Joshua's name had been submitted by Keith's parents, Vic and Elveda, to receive any wish he wanted. At first, I felt we did not deserve their offer and it embarrassed me. I had always taken pride in being able to support myself and finding ways to get what I wanted and needed on my own. It felt like a handout, and, for a moment, I let my pride and ego get in the way of their offer. I told them there must be many other families with more desperate financial issues who needed this opportunity for their own children. Though we had just built a new home and had our children in a private Christian school, we had put ourselves in great financial distress. Outwardly, though, it appeared we were in a much better situation and I assumed and hoped that was what the Make-a-Wish people would see.

I had long lived in denial about Joshua's illness and I wanted to maintain a façade of success. Allowing my pride to initially reject their offer, I could stave-off what was really happening. The deeper and more painful truth was I did not want to accept the meaning behind the wish they were offering: that my child had a terminal illness. I told myself it was far too soon, despite overwhelming medical evidence, to be certain of his diagnosis and I needed to see more proof of his physical decline.

I am uncertain if the Make-a-Wish folks saw through me and my flawed attempts to reject their offer. They were incredibly patient, generous, and persistent. They told me they did not choose recipients on the basis of a family's finances but were on a mission to create a wonderful memory for the entire family during a traumatic time in their lives. They convinced me our family was, indeed, deserving of their offer and they would be honored to be part of Joshua's wish. I understood and we set up an appointment to meet. We told them over the phone we had not yet told Joshua his disease was terminal and, in the difficult and heartbreaking years ahead, we never would tell him. It was a truth we felt he did not need to hear. I was committed only to help keep him mentally balanced even as his physical balance was faltering. We told him his muscles were not working as they should and that was a truth all of us could accept.

Sari and Michelle, our Make-a-Wish volunteers, arrived at the door with big smiles and gifts for both Joshua and Leah, a great icebreaker. The kids were excited and answered questions about their favorite toys, activities, and foods to eat. As Sari played with the children, Michelle sat with us and completed paperwork. I was impressed with their organization and the warm and welcoming environment they instantly created. When they asked Joshua "what he would do if he could do anything or go anywhere in the world," his answer was immediate: "I want to go to Disneyland." Keith and I always thought someday we would take our children there, but the previous two-and-a-half years were occupied with a very different journey. The joy on Joshua and Leah's faces when the wish-granters said: "OK! Let's plan it!" was truly priceless. We wept as we watched our children erupt in joy. They kept asking when we could go and when we could see Mickey Mouse, Donald Duck, Jasmine, and all of the princesses in Disneyland. Through two-and-a-half years of pain, sorrow,

 and reluctant acceptance of the truth, I felt a powerful moment of joy. The kindness of these strangers was an unexpected blessing and I vowed once more that I would someday pay it forward. Joshua continued struggling with his balance and energy levels and Sari and Michelle assured us they would

provide any medical equipment that might be needed to help him fully enjoy his upcoming adventure.

Three months later, on June 15, 1993, a sleek, white limousine pulled up in front of our house making us feel like royalty. Neighbors came out to send us off on our big adventure. At the airport, we were met by two Make-a-Wish volunteers who escorted us inside with balloons and backpacks filled with toys for the kids and activities and treats to keep them entertained on the plane. We were the first passengers ushered onto the Alaska Airlines jet, and Joshua and Leah were allowed to visit the cockpit and sit with the

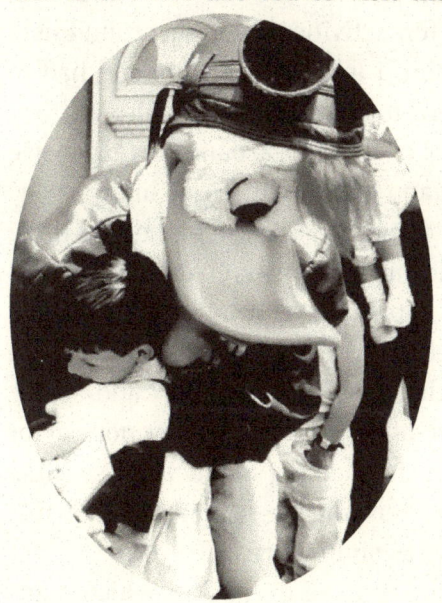

pilots for a few minutes before takeoff. Joshua got a pilot's pin that he later gave to his favorite Disney pilot character, "Launchpad McQuack." Before we took off, the pilot announced there was a very special guest on the plane, Joshua Chalcraft, heading to Disneyland courtesy of the Make-a-Wish Foundation and all the passengers applauded. I was surprised by the attention, elated for my children, and humbled once again by the kindness of strangers.

Keith's parents had driven from Seattle to Anaheim in their RV to join us on this family adventure. They were as excited as their grandchildren and wanted to be part of the fun after such a tumultuous and painful year. As we arrived at Disneyland, we were given a warm welcome and special buttons from Make-a-Wish. Just in case Joshua's little legs got tired, we were provided a wheelchair, but when Joshua saw it, he was adamant he did not want to use it, EVER! I told him he did not have to, but we needed it to carry our bags and other supplies and if he changed his mind, he could let me know. Leah, on the other hand, was thrilled with the wheelchair and wanted to sit in it immediately. Giving Joshua the choice to reject the wheelchair was the first of many times I would stand back and let my son fall in order to keep his dignity and give him the power to make his own choices. As difficult as that was and as much as we wanted to protect our little boy and keep him safe from harm, I knew he would need to learn to stand on his own in order to build his self-confidence and resilience. With all of the fun activities going on around us, I always kept one eye on him. I felt great anxiety and had to fight and overcome my need to control everything.

Within just 10 minutes of walking around the expansive Disney park, fatigue set in and Joshua whispered in my ear he wanted to sit just for a few minutes. For most of the next three days he needed the wheelchair, but was still able to enjoy all of the rides. Leah also complained of being tired and they would sit together in the chair. It seemed to be a way of being together and something that would build a new and strong bond between them. At five-and-a-half, I felt it was normal for her to get tired with all of the walking and activity swirling around her. I noticed that her gait was slightly off but told myself it was because she was simply tired.

We were ushered to the front of every line, which made me feel uncomfortable and, again, undeserving of this privilege. I could see parents trying to calm their cranky, impatient children who had been waiting for more than an hour to get on the rides. I looked sheepishly at one father standing near us with his small daughter and apologized for stepping in front of them. He looked at Joshua and Leah with great compassion and said, "You go ahead Mom, you've certainly earned it, and I would not change places with you for anything." It was the first time I realized how others saw us, that we were different. It was humbling to acknowledge the kindness of strangers, and I was grateful to hear this man's words. They gave me permission to accept his generosity without guilt. Again, I resolved to remember what this kindness felt like and committed to pay it forward whenever I could.

Joshua's adventure continued as we loaded into Keith's parents' RV and headed to SeaWorld in San Diego. Leah and her Dad sat in the front row of Shamu's fish tank and got splashed by his whipping tail. Her laughs and screams delighted me. Joshua was especially excited by the underwater glass shark tank. It was truly the trip of a lifetime and we spoke of it many times in the ensuing years. It was a momentary reprieve from the sadness of the previous years and brought much-needed respite, relaxation, and light into our family...light that would be dimmed in the near future.

With so much time and focus on Joshua, Leah was not getting the attention she needed and deserved. I met friends at the door of our home and asked them to acknowledge Leah first to make her feel significant. She had begun imitating Joshua's behaviors, falling, and saying she was tired. I chose to believe her actions were just an attempt to get more attention, to steal some of the focus from Joshua. Leah began to walk on her tiptoes with her knees distended, which was different from her brother's symptoms. When she fell, I brushed off her knees, cleaned her up and told her she would be fine. I was repeating a pattern of my parents' behavior with me many years earlier. But Leah was not going to be fine. And neither was I. I was terrified and could not allow myself to even imagine that my little girl could possibly have the same horrendous disease as her brother. This could not be happening again! The thought of that was beyond my ability to cope so I pushed the idea as far away from my mind as I could. In the safe place of denial and magical thinking, we chose not to get Leah tested. We decided just to wait and see.

What we could not avoid was how Joshua's friends and teachers were treating him differently and how much he resented that. He wanted to be seen as "normal," like all of the other kids. Sometimes he would intentionally misbehave in class just to get in a little trouble as the other children sometimes did. That ploy did not work well for him because he was, by nature, sweet, pleasant, and upbeat. Everyone loved him and forgave him, no matter what he did. What was becoming harder to avoid were Leah's symptoms, which persisted. Still, we decided to wait and try to determine if she was being authentic or imitating her brother. We were overwhelmed dealing with Joshua and could not face the prospect of having another child diagnosed with a terminal illness. I needed more time. I somehow instinctively knew the truth but could not bear to face it. I continued to attribute her symptoms as a ruse to get more attention and tried, as best I could, to make life for all of us as normal as possible.

Keith continued studying and teaching Bible classes at church and working full time at a health care facility. As if I was not busy enough caring for my own two children and maintaining my own household, I continued babysitting my girlfriend's two young boys, cleaning her home to earn extra money, and volunteering at church. I also kept occupied and distracted with my ever-growing Pampered Chef business. This was all exhausting but left no time for me to feel the sadness that threatened to overwhelm us every day. It was a comfortable and safe place for me emotionally. I was fixated on creating a new "normal" for my family and filling our home with joy no matter how much energy it took from me. I was trying with every fiber of my being to keep the darkness outside and bring in the light.

CHAPTER 6

The Day I Stopped Praying

"When a storm of devastation approaches you from all directions, it really knows your unlimited potential for fighting back"
—Mumtaz Kazmi

When Leah was six, I enrolled her in a ballet and tap-dancing class and often sat and watched her. She continued walking on her tiptoes and would often sit down and watch as others participated. Though she was a trooper and very much wanted to be part of the class, she often complained of being tired and had no energy to dance. I thought she was just being fussy, and I was, quite honestly, annoyed by her neediness.

One day her teacher approached me and asked if I had noticed that Leah's gait was different from the other girls. She told me that a couple of years earlier, she had a little girl in her class with a very rare neurological disease and that Leah seemed to exhibit similar symptoms. I froze. My heart seemed to stop beating and my eyes filled with tears as I stared at her. No sound came from my lips. She was saying things I did not want to hear. I wanted to grab Leah, run out the door as fast as I could and not listen to the words coming out of the teacher's mouth. She said it was "something Ataxia." My world stopped. In that instant I knew we could no longer deny what we most feared. We had to get Leah tested.

The neurologist at Seattle Children's Hospital already knew that Joshua had Friedreich's Ataxia and they had performed all of the required tests to confirm his diagnosis. After doing a minimal amount of testing on Leah in their offices, they scheduled a heart muscle biopsy to determine if she had hypertrophic cardiomyopathy, the final piece of a frightening medical puzzle that could determine if she, too, had FA. Since I did not expect any news that day, I told Keith it would be fine for him to stay at work and I would tell him about our visit to the hospital later that day.

I sat in the cold, dark waiting room in the basement of the hospital, sitting in fear on pins and needles, with my dear friend Pam, our pastor's wife. We waited patiently and prayed. I remember thinking they could cheer this place up a bit. Then the doctor came out with the sickening truth. My little fireball Leah, now six-and-a-half, had the same disease as Joshua. I was going to lose another child. I could not speak or think. I felt utterly powerless, completely abandoned by God and my depressed husband who was already shutting down trying to cope with Joshua's diagnosis. This news would completely destroy him. Pam drove Leah and me home and all I could do was hold her and let the tears flow as she slept on my lap. I was in shock and disbelief and when Leah awoke I sent her and Joshua upstairs and shared the terrible truth with Keith. As I feared, his depression deepened, but I had neither strength nor desire to help him in any way. I could not lean on or depend on him for any support and I had nothing left to give to him. We pulled further and further apart, both depleted, depressed, and distraught. I had two babies who needed me and would depend on me for all of the uncertain and frightening days ahead. Joshua and Leah were the only ones I could love, focus on, and care about.

Sometime after Leah's diagnosis, I remember driving on the freeway when out of nowhere I began yelling and screaming out a tortured pain emanating from somewhere deep inside me. It was a real, physical pain, an agony I had never experienced in my life. I felt desolate, helpless, power-less, and even ashamed, overcome with guilt that I had chosen to ignore Leah's symptoms when they first appeared a couple of years earlier. How could I have chosen to save myself from the truth at the expense of my little girl? Three decades later, I still have a lump in my throat and visceral pain in my heart as I release more tears writing this. I chose to think my little girl was simply vying for attention. By doing that, making that choice for my own survival, I had made her feel insignificant in much the same way my parents had made me feel as a child. I still carry guilt about the choice I made and will carry it for the rest of my life.

With two terminally ill children, I was now living with an unbelievable and indescribable pain of no one's making. I could only blame God, a God to whom, until that moment, I had devoted my life, a God to whom I vowed to be a good Christian, a God in whom I had faith and an unwavering belief. But now I had two children who were going to die young, and my faith wavered. But I could not let my faith die. I could not lose that. I had to hold on to my belief because it was the only thing I could control in that moment as everything else in my life was falling apart.

In the quiet of our home, Keith and I talked to the children and told Leah she had the same disease as her brother. As strange as it sounds, I remember seeing a small smile on her face. She seemed wholly unaffected by this news and simply asked if that meant that she, too, would get her own wheelchair someday. Her reaction shocked me as I now understood that she was realizing she would finally get the same kind of attention as Joshua, attention she desperately needed and craved.

That was the day I stopped praying.

I did not stop praying because I lost faith. I just could not reconcile having faith and hoping for a cure while simultaneously facing the reality I had to accept. How could I teach my children to accept their circumstances and pray for healing in the same breath? I had no time, no intention, no inclination to ask any help from God. I knew others were praying for healing, but in the reality of the life we were now forced to live and with the inevitable and terrifying ordeals that lay ahead of us, I did not have time to pray for a miracle. My challenge and energy now had to focus on raising my children, making them believe they were perfect and not broken, that they were not accidents of nature. If I prayed for something different, I felt it would be a betrayal of who they truly were. It made no sense for me to pray for a different outcome. If I could have found time to pray for anything, I would have prayed for God to give me the strength to get through the upcoming struggle. I knew I would never understand why God allowed this to happen, but I had to believe God loved us and there must be some purpose for this astounding tragedy that now defined our lives.

Over the next couple of months, though I was lost and spiraling downward, I kept my friends and family at a distance. I did not want comfort. I did not believe I could even receive it if it were offered. I feared I would disintegrate into ashes if I allowed myself to feel the depths of sorrow we were facing. How could this be happening to my family? I only wanted to sit in the darkness, hold my little children close, and pretend none of this was real. One evening, some weeks after Leah's diagnosis, three members of my "tribe" – April, Debby, and Amy – brought dinner to us. I met them at the door, still in an emotional fog, not ready to receive comfort from anyone. They planned to sit with us, intending to be a pleasant distraction, but I could not receive what they wanted to give. I think I thanked them for the food but sent them on their way. They would tell me later how incredibly sad and helpless they felt, knowing I must have been in a terrible place, unable to even sit with them.

Keith was a man who loved his children, but his despair and feelings of helplessness paralyzed him. He believed as the man of the house his role was to protect and provide for his family, but the hopes and dreams he had for his children were now crushed. He seemed unable to face a life where they would not be able to enjoy all the activities he loved. We clung to each other at night, desperate for comfort, but neither of us could give or receive support. I had two children as well as a husband who depended on me. My drive to survive was strong. Though I knew we would have to find some way to live in this new and frightening place, I was filled with anxiety and terrified about what the future held for us. The wise words of my friend came back to me once again. "You don't have to be ready for what tomorrow will bring, just focus on today and the things you must face now. Take one day at a time". I was also determined to follow the advice my father had given me and watch my children live, not watch them die.

CHAPTER 7

Denial to Acceptance

"The eye sees all, but the mind shows us what we want to see."
—William Shakespeare

In the aftermath of Joshua's and Leah's diagnoses, I could no longer deny what was happening. I never asked "why my children?" I remember thinking "even if God himself came down from the heavens, looked at me, and told me why, I doubt I would have believed a word, even coming from the mouth of God." I would never be able to accept a reason because there was none. No explanation would ever be good enough.

Instead, I began asking a different question: "How?" How can I be a great mother to my beautiful children? How can I be the mother they will need to help them survive and even thrive in the days they had remaining on this earth? How can I teach them they are not broken, not mistakes, or somehow less than full human beings? How can I guide them to find purpose and how can I help them to live their absolute best lives? How can I keep self-pity at bay, both for my children and for myself? The answers to all the "how" questions would be my guiding principles for the rest of our lives together. There was one remaining question: Will there ever be laughter and joy in our home again? I knew that answer. Yes...and it was up to me to make that happen. It was time to face our new reality, adjust our expectations of the future and accept, however reluctantly, our "new normal." There was no more time for sadness. It was too heavy a weight to bear.

Keith and I continued attending the annual national Ataxia Foundation conferences. The care and understanding of people who were in our same situation became a strong support system for us. At these meetings, we had a sense that we were not alone and could share the hardships and challenges we were facing openly and without hesitation. We established long term friendships that eventually connected our children with other children facing the same disease. As good friends watched our children, we traveled throughout the country to meet with doctors, scientists, and other families whose children were living with various forms of Ataxia, including people from the Seattle area.

Soon after Leah's diagnosis, I reminded myself of my promise to "pay kindness forward" and try to help others while helping ourselves. I formed a local chapter for all types of Ataxia and we began meeting at a local library monthly. I was surprised at how many families in our area were affected by this disease and it was both encouraging and comforting to know we were not alone. In the beginning we invited only parents to the meeting, wanting to give them an opportunity to share openly without concern for what their children may hear. Eventually some of the children joined in. Leah was eager to meet with other kids who faced the same illness. At times I invited guest speakers to talk about physical and occupational therapies to try, emotional wellness for the family as well as support services available for people with special needs. Periodically we would have a social potluck at my home which I always enjoyed. Even at the age of seven Leah got involved along with me in the Muscular Dystrophy Association. We participated in the MDA telethon as well as many other fundraising events. At that time they were the main source of research investigating Friedreich's Ataxia

Unlike his sister, Joshua was not the least bit interested in being involved with anything having to do with his disability. When I would ask if he wanted to join us at various events and activities related to FA, he emphatically said "NO!" He was desperate to feel normal and had not accepted that his health was declining. He refused to socialize with anyone in a wheelchair and was busy living his life with his "normal" friends. I watched as he hung onto the walls, furniture, and even to his friends for physical support. His friends accepted him as he was, assisted him, and expressed great enthusiasm and joy in being Joshua's little helpers. They even argued about whose turn it was to push Joshua in his wheelchair and those gestures created a deep bond between them. As it had been for me, denial was his safe place to be. I thought it best to let him stay there and give him whatever time he needed to accept what was happening in his young life.

Keith and I continued volunteering in many of the events and charities focused on children with disabilities: the Jerry Lewis Telethon and several Muscular Dystrophy Association fundraisers. As we got more involved, we met more families dealing with the same challenges we were facing. Many of the children soon became friends with our own kids. Other than going to an MDA summer camp every year, Joshua continued to fight for normalcy in his life and avoid any event focused on his disease. At camp, he felt normal since all the children had medical issues and many were in wheelchairs. I continued to encourage him to be who he needed to be and not try and rush him to accept anything he was not ready to accept. As soon as she was old enough Leah joined him at camp. All the children loved the freedom from their parents and loved all the activities planned to meet their needs.

The local Harley-Davidson chapter volunteered to give the campers rides in their sidecars. Entertainers and craftspeople came to camp and donated their time and attention to the children. These summer camps were a tremendous source of joy for the children and a chance for parents to take a much-needed break, if only for a short while.

I continued growing my successful Pampered Chef business, which provided a distraction as well as a sense of purpose not related to being a caregiver, mother, or wife. It also gave my family a financial boost. Focusing on my business saved me from losing myself and my mind. My travels to business conferences also gave me a break from my reality at home. Keith would have to be in charge, which was healthy for all of us. He loved his children and did a great job juggling his work and caring for Leah and Joshua. While I was away, the three of them had the opportunity to depend on each other without me there managing everything. It showed me I did not always have to be in control.

I eventually realized that because I always took charge, no one else had to. As a caregiver, this was a common, yet very problematic pattern. I was, in essence, enabling our unhealthy family dynamics. Still, when I returned home, I was unable to change my behavior. I was who I was but became more aware of the necessity to get away, for my own sanity and for the children and their father to bond.

When not focused at home with the children, Keith turned his attention to the church and his desire to become a pastor. It was something he had always wanted and was compelled to do from the day he went to a Billy Graham crusade and found God. Though my interest in being part of the church was waning, I wanted to support him and try, by doing that, to fight for our marriage. When a small church not far from where we were living needed a pastor, Keith applied for the position and was hired, though we were quite unprepared for what awaited us. Some members of the congregation felt completely abandoned by their founding pastor and had very high expectations for his replacement. It was a tense and unhealthy situation for us, but Keith was excited about this opportunity to fulfill his dream and ready to invest his time and energy into his new congregation.

My heart was no longer invested in pastoring a church. I told him I would encourage him, continue helping at home, and that I would go to church on Sundays. What I could not do was to take on any of the responsibilities of a typical pastor's wife. I would not lead the women's group, head-up the children's programs, or plan retreats. I lacked the energy for any of that and only had enough stamina to care for my children, my friends' two children, and my growing business. Although outwardly I seemed to be juggling things well, I hoped Keith would notice I was taking on too much and tell me to stop and just focus on the children, but he never did. Perhaps I was just putting on too good an act, to my own detriment. The truth that he never said anything, or seemed to notice anything, made me feel unloved.

Looking back, I can see that my expectation was unrealistic and unfair. It would have been more effective for me to initiate an honest conversation with Keith about my state of mind and my needs. I was not good at asking for what I needed. Hoping for a different result did not make it happen.

Joshua's and Leah's disease was slowly progressing and they were having increasing difficulty getting up and down the stairs in our home. It was 1994 and time to sell our lovely home in Maple Valley. We bought a nice, one-story house in Federal Way, Washington, close to the church where Keith was now a pastor. It seemed like a perfect place to raise our children. A nice, safe, quiet neighborhood with a beautiful Christmas tree farm across the street. The elementary school was four blocks away and school friends lived nearby. The design was unique with a beautiful glass arbor over the dining room. The hallway into the bedrooms was wide and would be easy to adapt the bedroom doors and closets for the kids' wheelchairs we knew would be necessary in the future. The bathrooms would need to be remodeled for accessibility, but that was not something we needed to do right away. It was a "tomorrow" issue that would take care of itself. There was a hot tub on the back deck to help ease the children's muscle pains. The house made me happy and soon felt like home. Happiness had been in short supply over the previous two years, so the prospect of this new home was a gift. We moved in just before school started and though Joshua and Leah were sad to leave their old school, they were excited about making new friends. I was also excited about moving. It was in my DNA from childhood to move around, meet new people, and have new experiences. More than anything, I hoped this would be a new beginning for my family who had already been through so much.

I watched Joshua and Leah as they began fourth and third grades respectively. I wanted to find a way to help them be accepted and respected at school by their teachers, but especially their classmates. My instinct sometimes was to try and minimize or hide the differences, but of course that doesn't work and only leads to further isolation. So once again I mustered up my courage, just as Keith and I had done when we first learned of Joshua's diagnosis and decided to stand before our church instead of retreating into our pain... only this time it was in the classroom.

I asked my children first and then their teachers if I could come and explain to all the children why Joshua and Leah seemed a little awkward when they walked. Their voices were beginning to slur and although they could still be easily understood, I knew children were sometimes cruel due mostly to ignorance and a lack of understanding. I hoped, by being allowed to explain what was going on, I could give my children support, spare them some further suffering, and help their friends understand.

In each classroom I introduced myself as Joshua's and Leah's mom. I asked whether they noticed my kids would sometimes step on their toes, bump into them, hang onto them, or lean on a wall to get from one place to another. They were shy at first, but soon said yes to all my questions. I assured them what my children had was not contagious and explained exactly what that meant. I said that FA was something they were born with and could not be passed on to anyone else. I said my children's muscles did not work properly and asked if any of them had broken an arm or leg. A couple of the students raised their hands and I asked them if those injuries made it difficult for them to do all the things they had done before. They began to understand a little bit about what Joshua and Leah were experiencing.

I asked them all to stand up, turn around three times, and then try to walk forward in a straight line. It was like a game for them and they did what I asked, giggling as they tried to walk forward, losing their balance, walking into each other, and bumping into their desks. When they finally sat down, I explained this was what Joshua and Leah experienced all the time. Their muscles did not work properly, which sometimes made them dizzy. I saw lights go on in their young minds and their fears of the unknown began to disappear. Then I shared a scenario I had earlier with my own children: I asked them to imagine four people who wanted to cross the street. One had a broken arm, another a broken leg, one was blind, and another in a wheelchair. Could they all cross the street? Some of the kids looked unsure and a few even said no. I replied they could all cross the street but would have to find their own way to do that. The blind person needed someone to help and possibly a cane. The person in the wheelchair would need to be pushed. The person with a broken arm could probably do it alone. The person with the broken leg would need crutches. No matter what, they could all do it. They just had to find a different way and rely on help from others. I was teaching life lessons that would become a way of life for me in the years ahead.

Within a year, Joshua entered fifth grade and the teachers

were telling us he was no longer safe at school. His symptoms were now much worse. He was falling more often and needed his wheelchair almost all the time. This was a turning point for all of us and saddened us deeply as Keith and I realized the disease was progressing. I was a long way from living in denial and, as my friend had said, I was prepared for the "momentous move ahead."

While it broke my heart to see Joshua fall, I worried more about the psychological effects these changes would have on him. I think, looking back at that moment when my children could barely walk on their own, Joshua was tired of not being able to keep up with his friends and seemed almost to enjoy the attention he got as his buddies argued over who would get to push him. The teachers finally created a schedule to decide who would push Joshua. His friends Brandon, Chris, Will, and Tommy all helped get him from one place to another. In helping and accepting Joshua just as he was, they became his lifelong friends.

Though his illness was terminal, we never talked about that, but focused on the life we had. Children are very intuitive and I knew they could deal with the truth easier than many adults did. It was better to address the issues and concerns with the classmates than ignore them and pretend they weren't real. The wheelchair that Joshua had once dreaded and resisted became, ironically, the very thing that bound him together with his friends.

Even though Leah seemed to envy Joshua's closeness to his friends, she was a very different child. He was an extrovert and wanted lots of friends around. She was his opposite and never enjoyed a lot of noise and activity. She lacked the confidence of her older brother. If there was more than one friend around, she felt excluded from conversations and uncomfortable competing for attention. She loved putting on plays at home, but always had to direct whichever friend was acting with her. This was her one way of trying to control her environment. She had to be the boss. Her friends did not always appreciate her pushiness, but they followed her lead. Quiet, little Karla became her "bestie" and they were inseparable for many years.

Because Joshua had paved the way for their mutual friends to accept their differences, Leah's friends never seemed to have much of a problem with any of her special needs. With both children, the disease was progressing very slowly and the subtle changes were not jarring to their friends. Unlike her brother, who did not want to acknowledge what was happening or be identified by his wheelchair, Leah seemed to enjoy the attention she got because of her wheelchair. I was incredulous at her behavior because I struggled accepting my little girl not being able to walk on her own. I actually resented her attitude and reaction to her illness. At the time, I could not understand her at all. I wish I would have understood and embraced her need to not only fit in but to stand out in a unique way amongst her peers.

Despite my hope that our new home would mark a new and happier beginning for our family, Keith and I were not doing well. Keith seemed quite content with me and often declared his love and appreciation, but I was no longer able to receive it. It was too late. Too much water under the bridge. I could not imagine staying in the marriage much longer, but also could not live with the pain I would cause my children if I broke up our family. Keith's depression and his negativity were becoming impossible to live with any longer. He seemed to be withdrawing more from me and the children, and I thought it was because he was so busy. In time, I would learn there was another explanation. He spent too much time sleeping and seemed more detached. When he was engaged, he wanted only to talk about what the kids could no longer do, such as picking up things and even losing the ability to write. I only wanted to focus on what they could still do and how pleased I was with the lives they were still able to live.

Talking about loss went against my desire to be optimistic and help them live the best life they could. This served me in some ways, but it took a toll on our marriage. I couldn't shift gears and join Keith's emotional space. I had to keep up the optimism or the whole thing would collapse. I witnessed many other marriages in crisis experiencing this same tension. Keith resented my decision to avoid talking about the reality of the kids' progression and one day, in a fit of frustration, accused me of not caring at all that our children's health was declining. His words both hurt and shocked me. I told him he needed to talk to someone else about this and not to me. I was going to focus on the positive. He could take his depression and negativity to a friend or his pastor. He apologized later for what he had said. He was just angry at what was happening to his children and felt helpless to save them from an inevitable and difficult future.

I am quite certain we both knew our marriage was on the verge of collapse, but he could not imagine I would ever leave. He held onto me tighter and the more he reached out, the more I pulled away.

Keith continued working as a technician at a healthcare facility and as a part-time pastor at his church. The tension was growing amongst the church members as it was in our home and we were not equipped to handle the problems at either place. Eighteen months after Keith began working as a pastor and after consulting with the senior pastor in our previous church, we disbanded the church and closed the doors. It was another traumatic and disappointing crisis for Keith, who now needed more of my attention, but I kept busy to help avoid time alone with him. The more he leaned on me, the more I pushed him away. I had no time, energy, or desire for him. I could only focus on my children and trying to create a new normal at least for the three of us. We stayed connected to our original home church and kept the children involved in various clubs there. This would be my last time as a member of a church. My faith in God remained strong but my belief in the traditional church teachings had diminished. Being a part of leadership over the years, I saw so much hypocrisy and contradictions and I needed to find my own way without being told what to say, do and believe.

As once before in an earlier failed marriage, I tried to eat my way out of my misery. At 38, I was now 80 pounds overweight and had lost sight of who I was as a woman. I was discouraged, ashamed, and angry at myself for allowing this to happen again. In taking care of Joshua and Leah, I had little to no energy to care for myself.

I realized I needed to change things, not just for me, but for the sake of my children. The first step of changing my life was recognizing the need to start with myself and take one small step at a time. It was difficult to put that first foot forward, but I knew it was the beginning of a commitment to live my life fully. I began the fen-phen diet, a combination of fenfluramine and phentermine. In the span of just four months, I lost all the weight and gained back my self-confidence. Though the drugs were taken off the market in 1997 after being linked to heart-valve problems, they worked wonders for me at a very desperate time in my life. It was like taking speed and I became almost machine-like, needing very little sleep, working on my business until the wee hours of the morning, then turning my attention to taking care of our home and the children. I was proud I was finally taking care of myself and applauded by my family and friends. I felt as if I had conquered a huge mountain and decided to create a bucket list of things I wanted to do in my life.

At the top of the list was the two-day Seattle-to-Portland (STP) bike ride. I began training with a couple of friends and was thrilled to focus on something fun just for me. Keith resented the time I took away from him and seemed to have no understanding about how much I needed to do this. We had terrible fights, but I was committed to doing what I needed to do for myself. I was elated when I crossed the finish line in Portland on a gray, rainy day. I had accomplished something I never thought I could do. It boosted my confidence and instilled in me a level of self-respect making me believe I could achieve anything once I put my mind to it.

Because this disease was progressive and terminal, I understood beyond any doubt that Joshua and Leah would never be as physically fit as they were at that moment. At the ages of 10 and 9, respectively, they were still able to do most of their activities, though were struggling more.

One thing Leah loved was participating in the "Dream On" beauty pageant for special-needs children two years in a row. "Dream On" was a non-profit organization founded by Angel Ward, Miss Washington USA, to allow girls with all types of special needs to participate in a beauty pageant. They were committed to helping these young ladies build self-esteem and confidence as they walked the runway and answered questions by judges. They also grant wishes to some of these contestants to create beautiful memories for the families. To Leah's delight, she was crowned both times she participated. The first year she was crowned "Miss Congeniality Dream On" and the following year she was named "Miss Pre-Teen Dream On." The first year she was escorted to the stage by a handsome young man and asked a question by the judges. I am not sure exactly what the question was, but I am sure her answer was "world peace." Both of these "wins" gave her attention and affirmation that she loved. Leah was a very pretty young girl with an infectious smile and a compassionate heart. I noticed when she was with other special-needs children, she was remarkably kind and patient. Despite her own disabilities, she always encouraged them and told them how pretty they were. After the pageant she would congratulate her competitors and tell them what a good job they had done. By the end of the second pageant, Leah was using her wheelchair most of the time, which she loved, and seemed to

Dream On pageant

adapt to it with few, if any, emotional problems or resistance. I believe she had great compassion for her brother and that, perhaps, her easy transition assured him he would not be alone in this battle.

Just as Make-a-Wish had done for Joshua, the Dream On Foundation granted a wish for Leah. She told them she dreamed of going to Mexico where she could swim in the warm water and soak up the sunshine. Within a couple of months, we were all off to Mazatlan, Mexico and treated with the same warm reception we received at Disneyland. Leah's hair was braided in true Hispanic style, and we visited a Mexican fiesta at the culture center. We watched her as she went tandem on a parasailing ride, pulled by a flimsy boat, flying high in the sky, feeling the wind blowing on her face. She was courageous and brave and it occurred to me my little girl was maybe more like I am than I thought possible. I was always ready and willing to try anything and I was so proud watching how daring she was. Joshua did not hesitate for a moment to decline the same offer. It was a wonderful trip, but the last vacation we would take as a family.

Keith withdrew more and slid into an even darker place. He was discouraged about the failure of the church and felt disconnected from the religious life he needed. The desire to be a pastor had been a driving force in his life for 20 years. Now he felt aimless and unsure how to move forward. He continued taking the kids to various activities at our previous church and cared for them when I was out of town for business. He took them fishing at nearby lakes and sometimes out to dinner and a movie. He loved them and they loved him, and he did his very best to provide for them. The struggles in our marriage had less to do with the children, I think, and more to do with his realization that I lost my emotional connection with him. I lost respect and trust in him somewhere along the way and that is why I felt the need to always be in charge. I stripped-away his ability to control anything. I had become hyper-aware of what the children needed, perhaps borne of the guilt I felt by missing the early signs of Leah's symptoms. I was not going to let that happen again.

I now see that excluding Keith and doing what I needed to survive daily life pushed him away further from Joshua and Leah as well. By shouldering so much of the day to day physical, emotional and medical needs of the kids, I enabled Keith to not take responsibility for being a strong father and husband. I was not helping build a strong family unit at all.

I had to try and create whatever happy moments I could. I knew my children would need their own "tribes" as they got older and invited their friends on family trips and to spend the night with us. I tried my best to fill our days with fun activities like going to the zoo, taking walks in the park, going to concerts, watching funny movies, and just hanging out at the beach. This was good for them and good for me. We had purchased the first of several wheelchair-accessible vans at great expense and told our friends and family they could borrow the vehicle any time they wanted. They rarely did and I understood they might be uncomfortable having Joshua and Leah with them in case anything out-of-the-ordinary happened. Some years earlier, before my children were diagnosed, my friend Amy asked me to watch her young toddler, Michael, who had severe Down syndrome. I told her "no" because I was nervous about something happening on my watch. My doubts about my ability to care for Michael helped me understand why others turned down my request to help with Joshua and Leah. It was a lot for anyone to handle.

Joshua was relying more and more on his wheelchair and we noticed changes in his feet. His high arches made it difficult for him to wear normal shoes and we had to buy shoes that were two sizes larger. This did not seem to bother our very fashion-conscious son, who loved wearing high-end designer clothing. Since we were not paying for tennis lessons, piano lessons, or sports equipment, we indulged both him and Leah in whatever clothes they wanted. It seemed a small-enough price to make them happy, and they were proud to be among the best-dressed kids wherever they were with their friends.

Because of Joshua's continuing problems with his feet, Seattle Children's Hospital sent us to Shriner's Hospital in Portland for corrective foot surgery. Once again, I had to watch my boy go through an incredibly painful ordeal with a long recovery period, which thankfully was successful. It allowed him to bear weight when we had to transfer him from his wheelchair to the toilet or to his bed. I was grateful for even these small victories.

The burden of lifting Joshua mostly fell on me. Because of the pain in his feet, Joshua was prescribed Oxycodone. I was feeling completely alone, both mentally and physically dis-tanced from Keith, and bore the burden of carrying not only my children's physical bodies, but most of the weight of their care. I was overwhelmed by what was happening to them. The only control I seemed to have was to manage their needs, feed them, and love them as best I could.

Though our marriage was in crisis, Keith tried to show me love by bringing me flowers, taking me out for dinner, praising me with compliments, telling me how beautiful I was, and what a great mother I was to the children. But it was too late. I heard him. I listened to him. But nothing he did or said got through. I had shut down and realized the stress of staying in the marriage caused more unhappiness than I could handle. We were both grieving, and grieving differently, and we found it impossible to give each other the love and comfort we both desperately needed. We were disconnected, done, and broken. Unable to find comfort with Keith, I went outside my home to help fill the emptiness inside of me.

Cliff and his wife were neighbors when Keith and I bought our first house. We sometimes ate meals together and their two daughters would babysit Joshua and Leah when they were babies. After we moved to our new home in Maple Valley, the home we built, we barely saw Cliff's family over the next several years. We reconnected when I was invited to their daughter's wedding reception. It was comfortable and easy being with Cliff again and I had always enjoyed his sense of humor and just talking with him. I had never had any romantic feelings towards him in all the years we had known one another. Now, he made me laugh again, something I missed terribly over the last several years.

We made a date for lunch so we could catch up and immediately formed a bond that we both needed and wanted. I was 39, rid of the 80-pound weight I had gained, and eager to see more of Cliff. I needed fun and laughter in my life and from our first reconnection, he provided both. Our marriages were in crisis. Cliff told me there was no love left in his 29-year marriage. We were in the same place, wanting comfort and change. For the next year we talked, listened, and began dreaming of a life together. We found the physical and emotional solace lost in our marriages, and the guilt we felt was not powerful enough to keep us apart. Still, the shame weighed very heavily on both of us, but we held on to each other nonetheless.

In the midst of the many crises in my life – my children's diagnoses, my illicit affair, and my crumbling marriage – I was turning 40, entering a new decade and decided to do something to counter all of the craziness. I decided to throw myself a party. I wanted to celebrate my friendships and be celebrated so I began organizing my guest list, sending out invitations, finding a venue, and making decorations. The party was something to look forward to, something that would bring some light into my life. My friends and family arrived from Canada and as far away as Quebec. We danced, ate, sang a little karaoke, and at the end of our song fest, my 11-year-old Leah took the mic and sang one of our favorite songs, *Roots and Wings* by Helen Reddy. I was moved to tears. I felt blessed, but only for a short time.

As soon as we arrived home after the party, Keith stole my joy. He accused me of being too wild at the party and not being a good Christian witness. Family and friends staying with us heard all of it and told me later they never liked the way Keith treated me. After his verbal assault, I could hardly stand being around him. My former in-laws, George and Lucille Kozub, left the next day to drive back to Canada but were so worried about my well-being they turned around, came back, and stayed in their RV in our driveway to ensure I was okay. They were worried about my emotional safety, having heard and seen too much. I knew I needed professional help.

I began seeing a therapist to try and figure out what I should do. She told me I was heading towards a nervous breakdown and needed a break from my husband and children for at least a few weeks to try to figure out what I truly wanted and needed to do. Keith agreed, realizing how critically important it was for me to take this step. I moved in with friends and within a day became physically ill. The stress I was under caused a severe kidney infection that took weeks to recover from. I was very sick, and while Cliff was concerned about my health, Keith was more concerned about the difficulty of caring for Joshua and Leah by himself. After I felt better, I went home every day to meet the children after school and spend time with them until Keith got home from work. Keith tried to be supportive, hoping I would come back feeling renewed, refreshed, and ready to rebuild our marriage. But the toll on my mind, body, and soul was steep and the damage irreparable.

If I was to survive and be the mother I needed to be for my children, I had to make drastic changes. During so many trials and the inevitable grief of watching my children's disease progress, I found it difficult to even see my own needs, much less care for them. I got lost in my children's needs and in a failing marriage. Great power and clarity came when I finally accepted the reality of my children's prognosis and began focusing on moving forward. I realized that if was going to watch my children live, not die, I would need to do the same for my own life. I had been dying inside the marriage. I had lost the weight and created the bucket list, but now it was time to accept that the marriage was over and I had to take the reins and become determined to live, not die. I learned the vital lesson of the importance of self-care. It was okay to be "selfish." I needed to take care of my children's mother – me – and acknowledge my own needs. I realized I would have to make changes, not only in my body, but in my whole life if I was going to survive and thrive in the next chapter of my life. I had to take difficult steps for my sake and for the sake of my children. As the saying goes, "you cannot change what you do not acknowledge." I acknowledged it.

The best day ever!

CHAPTER 8

Fractured

"If you're going through hell, keep going."
—Winston Churchill

Though I was physically better, with my kidney infection cured, mentally and emotionally I was a wreck. I was still living away from Keith and the children and continuing to see my therapist every week. I was struggling with an impossible dilemma...how to find some happiness for myself without causing harm to my children.

I knew I needed to take care of myself before I could care for others. The idea of focusing on myself went against everything I had been taught as a child, believing you always had to put others first and doing anything else would be considered selfish. How could I be the mother I needed to be when I was withering away inside? My therapist suggested I invite Keith to join our next session. He had been seeing my therapist's husband, also a therapist. I assumed they had talked about us, unsure of the protocols involved in discussing clients. They believed a meeting between Keith and me would bring about some sort of resolution. Keith and I were both nervous. My stomach was in knots because I knew I would have to reveal my affair with Cliff, though at that moment I did not know Keith had his own secrets.

We sat down, looked at one another and Keith began by

saying he still loved me. He had been saying that to me all along, but his words never matched his actions. To me, it felt as if he was really saying "I want you" as if he needed me to do things for him, to take care of the house and the children. If he did love me, it was hardly unconditional and our discussion quickly went downhill.

He confessed he had fallen back into his old drug habit, this time stealing prescription drugs from the healthcare facility where he worked and from Joshua's Oxycodone foot surgery prescription. This, he said, had been going on for the past two years. Keith's revelations finally made sense to me. I remembered wondering why Joshua ran out of his meds so quickly, worrying why Keith seemed to be sleeping so much, and watching Keith become more and more disengaged from our family. The telltale signs were there, but I was either too busy to recognize them or, perhaps, I chose to deny or ignore what was happening. Sitting beside me on the therapist's sofa, Keith acknowledged the damage he had done to his family and promised he would do better in the future. He apologized over and over, but I was enraged. He was "so, so sorry," but once again his words meant nothing to me. He promised to get more help by going to a church-related Celebrate Recovery program. He continued to tell me he still loved me and wanted to work on our marriage. Keith's deception about his drug use, stealing drugs from his own son and from his workplace seemed truly unforgivable. His professed love for me rang false. His confession about his drug use was true, something I could not deny. My children's father was a drug addict. But Keith was not the only one with secrets.

It was my turn to confess I was having an affair and had been deceiving Keith for the past year. I told him how miserable I was in our loveless marriage and lonely I felt living with him. I did not love him anymore and told him I wanted a divorce. I began to realize we were both coping with our struggles by finding the comfort we both desperately needed outside our marriage. Keith turned to drugs. I turned to a person who loved and truly cared about me. Realizing we had both lied and deceived each other helped temper my anger towards Keith. He begged me to give him another chance. Though I knew I could never love him or even like him again, I knew I could no longer live without my children. They needed me. I needed them. After being gone for two months, I went home.

For the next few days, he became a different person—attentive, understanding, and caring—the husband I had always wanted. He had been that way on-and-off throughout our marriage, so I knew he was capable of being a good man. Though we slept in the same bed, I made it clear we could not be intimate. I came back to try and be friends with Keith and knit our family together as best I could.

Joshua and Leah were thrilled to have me home, but I saw immediately the toll my absence had taken on both. They looked tired and there was no joy in their young faces. The childlike innocence there before I left was gone and my heart broke for them. Keith and I talked about what went wrong in our marriage—the broken promises, the failure to communicate, too many fights, and the recognition we wanted each other to change—a hopeless expectation. We talked about what our future might look like if we stayed together. Keith said all the right things, forgave me for my affair, and promised to be a better husband, but his words still meant nothing to me. Meaningless. I did not trust him. Within a week of moving back home, the fighting and arguing erupted again. He wanted to know where I was going and what I was doing. He was once again trying to control me. Though I kept my promise not to see Cliff again, Keith was jealous and insecure and said he could not trust me. My affair devastated him and seriously damaged his ego. He was striking out at me and it was abundantly clear he had not forgiven me. I could not forgive his lying about his drug use and lost my trust in him. I could not forgive myself for my own deceptions and could not live this way any longer. Again, I told Keith I could not stay in the marriage.

I sat with Joshua and Leah in their bedrooms, held them tightly, and with tears in my eyes told them I would be back, but for that moment I had to leave. I could not stay with their father any longer. My words broke their hearts and mine as well. And yet I knew without a doubt that leaving the marriage was the only way I could stay true to my determination to watch all of us live, not die. If I had stayed, I would have to become dead inside. I couldn't do that to myself or to my children.

I left Keith and my children again and fled to a place where I knew I would feel safe.

Without warning I knocked on Cliff's door and asked him, "What are you doing for the rest of your life?" He began sobbing, opened his arms, and took me in. We held onto each other for a long time, both needing love, support, and comfort. He listened without judgment, let me cry when I needed to, and continued to remind me of all the amazing things he loved about me. He gave me a shoulder when I had no one else to lean on and reassured me all would be well...eventually. I had no idea what the future might hold for us or how I could be with my children again, but for that moment, I found a place where I felt safe and secure.

Keith retaliated in the cruelest way. He took out a restraining order against me, claiming I was an unfit mother. I was no longer allowed to pick up the children from school. He changed the locks on our doors and threw my personal belongings on the front lawn of our home for all the neighbors to see. He shamed me in front of everyone we knew and most of our friends from church shunned me. Other than when our children were diagnosed, this was the lowest and most painful moment of my life.

Incredibly, even after all we had been through, Keith

continued telling me he loved me and wanted me back, but now he committed an unforgivable sin. He told 12-year-old Joshua and 11-year-old Leah about my affair and shared with them how devastated he was by what I had done. He turned my own children against me and did something no parent should ever do: involve children in adult problems. If there had ever been hope of a reconciliation, this was the deal breaker. With the children now dragged into the chaos of our marriage, I had to leave, but found myself torn again, conflicted and confused about what to do.

I could not stop thinking about my children and how I could make life better for them. Joshua and Leah were angry with me and blamed me for tearing our family apart and had no idea why this was happening. As mothers so often do, I had sheltered them from the rancor and turmoil between Keith and me. In their reality, everything seemed fine. Whatever they had witnessed seemed normal in their world. Now their seemingly safe place and once-happy home was destroyed and in their young minds it was my fault because I was the one who was leaving. They rejected me and their anger filled me with unbearable guilt. How could I have done this to them? How could I save myself and take care of my own needs without depriving them of theirs?

While the breakup of any family can be damaging to children, in my case I had been warned that excessive stress could cause Joshua's and Leah's illnesses to progress more rapidly. It was an impossible place to be with no easy way to escape. Keith continued pleading for me to return, but I could not go home again. I went back and forth. Break ups can often be messy like this, but ultimately it was clear the marriage was over and we were finally divorced.

The next time we went to court, I signed the papers without shedding a tear. Our marriage was legally over. I thought about my struggle the first time we stood before a judge and why I cried uncontrollably. I was mourning the loss of my dream of a happy marriage and an intact family for my children, but not regretting the loss of this man.

I kept our house and Keith kept our other assets. I encouraged him to use the special van we had bought for our children and even stay in the house when it was his weekend to have the kids. I could stay with Cliff on those weekends. Our new normal began and our arrangement worked for several months, but Keith's relationship with Joshua and Leah was inconsistent. Some months he was attentive, helpful, and fun and other times he would isolate himself, be dismissive, and sometimes choose not to see the children at all. I never knew what to expect from him or what person was going to show up, and this kept the children and me off-balance.

I was free from a miserable marriage, but not from the guilt of having an affair and the burden I still felt for breaking up our family. I found myself apologizing to Keith repeatedly for the affair, though in time I realized what I truly needed was to forgive myself.

After the divorce, I again tried to establish a new normal for my little family. I was a single mother, still dating Cliff, and trying to revive my Pampered Chef business that had all but collapsed in the craziness of the previous two years. I was barely able to make ends meet. Keith's child support payments and the little income I had at the time from my own business were insufficient to cover my bills. For the second time in my life, I found myself standing in line at a food bank and asking for help paying a long-overdue electric bill. The people at the food bank sent me to various local churches asking for help getting vouchers to pay the electric bill. Some of these churches were familiar to me, places I had visited in the past. It was humbling and hurt my pride to do it, but I had no choice. The food bank promised to match any money I raised on my own. It made me feel fragile and vulnerable, but also grateful that my pride did not get in my way of doing whatever I needed to do to take care of my children.

While I managed to take care of us financially, money could not solve the emotional problems in our home. Joshua and Leah, now 13 and 12, felt the sting of divorce as many children do. They loved both Keith and me, devastated as their safety net disappeared. They struggled to remain loyal to us both and, inevitably, felt pulled in two directions. Joshua was especially angry because he adored his father and continued blaming me for Keith's leaving. He wanted to be just like his father, unaware of his father's worst behaviors, only seeing him as the dad he loved. Leah, on the other hand, was sad, but not nearly as devastated as her brother. Keith never really paid as much attention to her as he did to Joshua. She had always felt second best.

Within six months of our divorce, Keith married a woman he had been seeing during our separation. They got married in secret somewhere out of state. Leah was particularly devastated at not being included in her father's decision. To her, it was another form of rejection. Keith's new wife, Jill, was struggling with her own addiction to methamphetamine, which became a huge source of contention between Keith and me. I desperately needed respite from caring for our children and trying to revive my business, so I let Keith continue to have the kids every other weekend though it terrified me to let them go. The children both knew about Keith's and Jill's drug use. Joshua thought it was cool, but it made Leah very uncomfortable. She did not feel safe and often begged me not to make her go. Still, she wanted to see her dad, and Joshua would argue with me if I even hinted at not letting them go. I worried about their safety when they were not home with me, but I was exhausted from battling the kids and worrying about Keith's and Jill's drug use. I needed respite to replenish my energy and there was no one else to care for the children. I let them go to their father and hoped and prayed he would keep them safe.

CHAPTER 9

Unbroken

"Being challenged in life is inevitable, being defeated is optional."
— Roger Crawford

I was finally free from a troubled, miserable marriage. Getting divorced was the most deliberate, dramatic, and consequential step I took towards self-care. We all adjusted slowly to our new lives. If I thought my new freedom would give me full control of our lives, it was an illusion. I think it was something I told myself to live with the reality that so much, perhaps most, of our lives were so out of our control.

The guilt and shame of breaking-up our family continued to haunt me and both children continued to express their unhappiness with my decision to break up our family which led to divorce. Joshua said repeatedly he wanted his dad to come back and blamed me for messing-up everything.

Change – especially a divorce – can be tough for any child, but even more challenging for children with special needs. Having a routine, a predictable, reliable way of life, was Joshua's comfort zone, his safe place. Leah seemed less rattled and more accepting of how unhappy I was. Though she loved Keith, she told me it was obvious her father and I were not happy together. Joshua and Leah were becoming teenagers and even without having to deal with a divorce they would likely be complaining about something. I was determined the pain I had caused our family would not stand in the way of my commitment to be happy. I vowed to use everything in my power to make every moment I had with Joshua and Leah as wonderful as possible. I had no idea how much longer I would have either one of them, but I knew there was no time to waste.

As we settled into our "new normal," I continued refocusing on my Pampered Chef business. I began recruiting consultants for my business and continued supporting my existing team. The Pampered Chef is a direct-sales company with each consultant basically self-employed. I was paid on commission based on personal sales and as a director, I earn a percentage of our teams' sales. The more consultants I was able to hire, the greater my income. The most common way to promote sales was hosting cooking parties in people's homes. I love to entertain, something I inherited from my mother. She taught me how to create a nice table and how to make guests feel special. It was a perfect fit for me, both emotionally and financially. My business allowed me to work late at night once the children were in bed and on weekends, hosting home parties when they were with Keith. I loved the interaction with complete strangers and my guests seemed to enjoy coming to the parties. It was fun, entertaining, and a big boost to my self-esteem that had been whittled-down after my life with Keith. Inevitably it was sometimes exhausting, but I was determined to make this work to give us the best life possible.

All my hard work paid off when I was promoted to the position of executive director in 2013 with about 400 consultants reporting to me. I loved what I was doing. It not only gave me financial security, but opportunities to travel and, perhaps most importantly, a sense of purpose and accomplishment as a businesswoman. Being self-employed gave me the flexibility I needed to spend time with my children as well as my ability to provide well for them. Once my financial incentives moved beyond survival, my incentive to work hard and succeed was the desire to travel with and expose them to as many activities as I could. I was trying to cram as much life and joy as possible into whatever time remained. In this way we were all committing to living our best lives now and not fretting about what the future would bring.

Even so, my commitment for all of us to live as healthily and happily and fully as possible every day, couldn't stop Joshua's and Leah's disease from progressing. Their diminishing physical abilities meant they needed help to do almost everything. Alone, in the quiet of my bedroom, I mourned and grieved each loss as I am also certain did my children. The most difficult loss was their ability to walk on their own.

When the day finally came that both my children needed wheelchairs, I was able to cope with this new challenge by putting a positive spin on it for their sake. I told them the wheelchairs would help them maintain more independence and allow them to keep up with their friends. Joshua and Leah, now 13 and 12, picked-out the colors of their new wheelchairs and added personal stickers wherever they wanted. They were also losing coordination with their hands and the ability to write, which made taking notes at school nearly impossible, and I met with their teachers to find solutions to help them overcome that challenge.

Focusing on solving their problems rather than what they could no longer do seemed the best way to help and the best way to keep my sanity as the primary caregiver. I made sure they were both assigned peer helpers at school who used carbon paper when taking notes, giving one set to each child and keeping a set for their own use. As they moved into high school, the para-educators helped them in class with note taking, moving between classrooms as well as with personal care needs like using the bathroom. I made certain they were placed in the front of their classrooms so they could see and hear better. The hearing devices we tried failed, making every word coming from their teachers' mouths sound like echoes. I arranged for all their tests to be done orally since they were no longer able to use their hands to write. Joshua was self-conscious, resisted help, and told me how much he hated having a para-educator. It made him feel "special and different," a category he abhorred. At times he would look for any chance to slip away from his helper to maintain his sense of independence. Leah, on the other hand, appreciated the help and the companionship.

I hoped staying positive and upbeat would inspire the same reaction in my kids and, fortunately, they often followed my lead. Their teachers and friends seemed impressed by their attitudes. I put a huge effort into ensuring they did not develop a chip on their shoulders. I wanted them to learn how to face challenges and working through them was a way to build self-confidence. I wanted to teach them the world owed them nothing and we get what we give. Sometimes I had to let them fail in their efforts to deal with their disabilities, but I knew from my own childhood that falling and getting up again made me stronger and more resilient. As their mother, sometimes I wanted to pick them up and do everything for them, but I resisted that urge. It was tough and painful for me to watch them struggle, but necessary for them. Just as they seemed to overcome each obstacle, life continued...unrelenting...throwing barriers into their paths.

Joshua and Leah developed scoliosis, the result of living fulltime in their power wheelchairs. The doctors at Seattle Children's Hospital told me this would become a life-threatening condition that could eventually cause suffocation and needed to be corrected soon. They recommended we proceed with full spinal fusion surgery with a Barrington rod, a stainless-steel spinal instrument implanted in the spinal column to treat curvatures. This would help them maintain good posture. Their backs would be opened, their spinal vertebrae fused together, and the rod laid alongside their spine from the neck down to their tail bone, down one side and up the other. It would be painful and require up to three months recovery. Besides the spinal surgery, Leah needed corrective foot surgery. Like Joshua, her foot position dropped, turned inward, and pointed downward, making it almost impossible for her to wear normal shoes. The doctors said they could do both surgeries on her at the same time and do Joshua's procedure too.

I would be the primary caregiver during recovery and made the decision to do everything at once, both children's spinal surgeries and Leah's foot surgery. It was the only way I could imagine having the energy to care for them, though I was nervous about being a single mother, able to help two kids recover at the same time. I had confidence in the doctors but was still frightened at the prospect of them getting anesthesia, given their heart problems. It is common in all children with FA to have hypertrophic cardiomyopathy, a thickening of the left ventricle of the heart that causes tremendous strain on the heart muscle.

Despite the emotions with which we were all dealing, over a period of three months their recovery went well. As they were improving, my anxiety and sadness were diminishing, which was a good thing because their physical needs required virtually all of my attention and energy.

They were so brave, rarely complained, and, thankfully, slept a lot during the first few weeks of recovery. It never really occurred to me that I could not lift my 100-pound children. It was never a choice, never an option. I just did it. It was what I had to do. As I had done when they were younger, I read to them both, which they loved. When their friends from school came over to visit, I got a bit of a break. Their teachers sent their assignments home so they did not lose too much ground academically.

Both spinal surgeries were successful and they were able

to sit much straighter in their chairs without fear of ending up crouched for the rest of their lives. Leah's recovery from her foot surgery was far more difficult and painful. The pain in her feet caused her to curl her knees up to her chest and she lost the ability to completely straighten her legs. The surgery was supposed to correct her foot positioning as Joshua's surgery had, but Leah was not so fortunate and the never-ending pain eventually meant she was unable to bear weight on her feet again. She had to be lifted every time she needed to get in or out of her wheelchair. Joshua was still able to put weight on his feet, just needing to be held up and pivoted onto his bed or toilet.

As the children continued losing their physical abilities, I somehow became both physically and mentally stronger and more resilient. I managed to keep my focus on the positive side of every challenge that arose and be grateful for the life we had. I chose gratitude and told my kids it was very difficult, nearly impossible, to be grumpy and grateful at the same time. Even watching my children's disease progress, I was nevertheless content with my life and found untapped strength inside me to keep moving forward. Cliff and I continued to see each other when possible and he began coming to the house to see Joshua and Leah as well. Joshua was not kind to him and blamed him for the divorce. I understood my son's attitude and did not try to force him to accept my relationship with Cliff. I believed time would eventually heal this rift.

As our need for care and assistance increased, I petitioned the Washington State Department of Social and Health Services to designate and cover the cost of more care hours for both children. Caregivers have to be experts at investigating and gathering resources that are available to them. This can take time but educating myself about what help was available was crucial. I was determined to give my children and myself the best life possible and that motivated me to become particularly good at this. I began searching for a part-time caregiver, someone who could work with all of us. I was mostly concerned for Joshua's and Leah's social and emotional needs, but also someone I was comfortable having in our home. I wanted a young person with a positive outlook on life and an interest in the medical field who would be comfortable doing some physical therapy, bathing, and feeding my hungry teenagers. I was unsure how to even begin such a search, but one day it occurred to me to contact our local college to try and find a student in the physical and occupational therapy department.

Tammi was an answered prayer, lacking in practical experience, but making up for it with a beautiful heart and willingness to learn. The kids loved her. She was funny, relaxed, and ready to help them with whatever they needed. At first, she was scared about picking them up from their wheelchairs, hoping and praying she would not drop them. Joshua and Leah initially resisted her help, feeling safer with me doing everything for them. But they eventually learned to trust her and she became part of our family for the next two years.

On Leah's 13th birthday, I noticed she was constantly asking for water and urinating a lot. She was lethargic and appeared unwell. I had seen these symptoms in Alex, one of the little boys for whom I had cared, and suspected what was wrong. After rushing her to the hospital, she was diagnosed with diabetes. Adding to everything else, she now required two insulin shots a day and her blood sugar levels monitored before every meal and bedtime. This new routine would last for the rest of her life.

Leah amazed me with her courage facing yet another new challenge. She was nervous at first about the daily shots, but quickly adjusted to doing whatever was necessary. It was not as if she never complained, but as I had previously told Joshua, being brave doesn't mean it is wrong to be afraid. It means facing what frightens you and doing it anyway. Leah did that and so did I. One more thing to face, reckon with, and find the will to go forward. We were becoming warriors.

My teenagers had obstacles most young people never face, but I could not let those barriers keep them from having healthy social lives. I encouraged and even pushed them to try various activities and clubs at school. I also planned road trips for us as a family to Kelowna and Calgary, Canada. We cranked-up the music on the radio and stopped for food and bathroom breaks along the way. I became an expert in navigating wheelchairs in and out of just about anywhere and remarkably creative in working out any complications we faced.

Consistent with the early days of the diagnoses, I never asked "why" we were facing so many obstacles, only "how" we could overcome them. I figured out early on that asking "why" us immediately made me feel like a victim of some cruel life twist or some mean God punishing me. It felt disempowered and did nothing to help me or my children face what we had to face. But whenever I asked "how" I could overcome the obstacles we face, it lit up my fierce determination, my creativity and my will to live life fully.

We learned to laugh instead of being angry with bathrooms that did not have wheelchair access. Many times I had to lift both of them from their chairs and carry them to the toilets. When this happened, Leah did not hesitate for a moment to criticize managers and employees if their businesses did not provide reasonable access for people in wheelchairs. People illegally using handicapped parking spaces were also not exempt. One time Leah made her caregiver pull up behind a car parked illegally and basically gave the driver "hell" when she came out to leave. The woman said she was helping a friend in need, but Leah was having none of it. She had heard that story before and was not buying it. "Shame on you for taking a space meant for someone like me and we could call the police on you." She laughed when she recounted this story, but I could see how empowering it was for her to stand up for herself and for others. She was always an advocate for those with special needs.

Given my "watch them live" motto, whatever my children wanted to try I found a way to make it happen. When Leah wanted to go ice skating, I pushed her in her chair on the ice so she could feel the experience. When Joshua wanted to play pool, Keith took him and some of his friends to a pool hall and held the stick while his son pushed the cue forward to hit the ball. I never asked if something could be done, only "how can we make it happen?"

I needed and managed to take a couple of short, personal vacations every year as my dearest friend, "Auntie" Wanda, came to watch the children. She loved them dearly and they loved her. She was nervous at first, worried about how to manage if the kids needed something, but I left her with a 10-page manual listing everything they could possibly need or want and how to provide it. We later laughed about the details I had given her, but she was grateful for the guidance. She also knew Keith was available if, by some chance, I had left out information she needed. Over the years, she would be a saving grace for all of us, her love and devotion unparalleled. It's said it takes a village to raise a child and an entire city to raise children with special needs. Wanda made so many things possible for us. She loved to shop and so did Leah and shopping trips became "their thing."

PART THREE

CHAPTER 10

Joshua's Journey – Teen Years

"You can't go back and change the beginning, but you
can start where you are and change the ending"
—c.s. lewis

As Leah and Joshua began their ninth and tenth grades in high
school, I noticed changes in their behavior, more than what
would be considered normal anxiety for teenagers in a new
school. Their old friends from middle school were easily
finding new friends with new interests and joining groups that
often did not include Joshua and Leah. They seemed detached
and isolated from their friends and looked for ways to
integrate into a new place with new people who had never
dealt with kids in wheelchairs.

Craving social interaction with other kids, Joshua tried to
fit in. Though he could not play football, he wanted to be part
of the team and asked the coach if he could be an assistant and
the coach and team welcomed him. This was one way he could
be around his buddies. They seemed to love having him as
their very enthusiastic cheerleader, but they would do other
things off the field and go their own way, which often did not
include Joshua.

In class, he made improper remarks at inappropriate
times and enjoyed when other students laughed at him. He
thought it was funny and though the teachers loved him, they

were not at all pleased at how disruptive he had become. He raced his power wheelchair down the halls at school and often jokingly bumped into people. "Oops" became his favorite word and he continued to enjoy the attention he was getting from his disruptive behavior. He wanted and enjoyed the attention he received, but for all the wrong reasons. He ignored teachers when they hollered at him to slow down and thought these moments were funny and just kept going. At parent-teacher conferences, we were told Joshua was not learning well in his regular classes and they recommended special-education classes where he could receive more personal help. He fought back hard against this solution and said he would refuse to go to school if he had to go into classes for special-needs kids. I had to force the issue, but after meeting with some of the teachers and beginning Joshua in a writing program, he adjusted to this new challenge. He was desperate to belong somewhere, to fit in with someone, anyone who would accept him.

Sadly, it was the kids doing drugs behind the school who welcomed him into their group. They made him feel as if he was one of the "cool" kids. Joshua knew about his father's drug use and began smoking pot and drinking alcohol. After all we had been through, after all we had overcome, I was angry seeing him waste his precious life doing such harmful things. He did not seem to care about anything and seeing my sweet, funny, kind little boy turn into a hoodlum with a bad attitude sickened me. He ignored what I said, disrespected me, and called me stupid for criticizing him. The more I tried to stop him the harder he pulled away and fought me. The day he called me a bitch, I slapped him in his face. It was the first and only time I ever hit my son. It not only shocked him, but it also stunned me and I knew I needed help for my son. Parenting a teenager under normal circumstances brings many challeng-es...parenting a teenager with disabilities brings an additional set of very difficult challenges. Watching Joshua go through rebellion and explore recreational drugs and alcohol frustrated me to my core. Knowing the medical/physical consequences of risk behaviors could be far more dire than with other teenagers and wanting my son to live as long as he possibly could, drove me to search desperately for solutions. I took him to private counseling for several months, which he completely resisted, resulting in little effect on his attitude or his behavior.

As a mother, I did not know how to deal with this, but other authorities did. One day, while he and his new derelict friends were in the back of the school smoking pot, security came around and found them. His "buddies" dumped their pot and beer into Joshua's backpack attached behind his wheelchair and took off. Joshua did not know where to go and remained, uncertain what to do next. He was handcuffed, and the authorities called me and asked me what to do with him.

He was 16 and could have been booked for possession of marijuana. I told them to do whatever they would do with any other student. Joshua always wanted to be treated as normal, like all the other kids, and this seemed like a good time to give him what he wanted. I had always allowed my children to suffer the consequences and enjoy the rewards of their actions and this was one of the hard consequences I had to allow my son to experience, no matter how badly I wanted to protect him. This was part of teaching them to become mature and mentally healthy, strong and responsible people. My hope was that he would learn life lessons from this experience. He seemed elated when they filed a report requiring him to go to drug counseling classes and disappointed when they did not take him to jail. He wrongly believed that would be a claim to fame.

I did not know how to help him. He was angry at home and fighting with me about everything. For the first time in years, I felt powerless, hopeless, and helpless. In truth, I just did not want to deal with this. I just wanted him to snap out of it and go back to being a nice boy. I took him in for weekly counseling sessions that didn't seem to help. Keith, as usual, was not much help, either, because he was still struggling with his own addiction and believed, naively, Joshua would grow out of it. Leah was 16 and also frustrated with her brother's attitude and tried talking to him. He pushed her away as well. He was angry with the life he was living and felt stuck and stifled with few options to change things.

One day, shortly after turning 18 and a senior in high school, I told Joshua he did not have any real friends because they were tired of listening to him talk about drugs and had moved on to other more interesting people and activities. I reminded him that the people he thought were his "real friends," the drug users, had abandoned him on the day of the drug bust, and were not true friends. I told him it was up to him to choose a different way to live if he wanted a better life. He just sat there staring at me and I wondered if he even heard what I was saying. I now know that he took my words to heart.

Keith, now drug-free and leading a recovery program at church, took him to a church youth group where he met Pastor Paul McArthur, just the right person to come into Joshua's life at that moment, someone who would have a huge, important, and positive impact on him. I believed that finding his faith and hanging around a group of young people who were also searching would be a positive step forward for Joshua and I was grateful. Pastor Paul treated him like a normal boy. He was sharing God's love in action and encouraged Joshua to attend the church recovery program and join in the youth group activities. Within a few months Joshua, by the grace of God, found the strength to leave his life of drugs behind and began dedicating his life to serving God. Whatever life remained for my son, this was a miraculous turning point for him and for all of us. In August 2003, Joshua gave a speech to his youth group at church. Here is part of what he said:

"I know God loves me because I used to do drugs and I was

heading down the wrong path, but then something happened and I found God. I had a dream and it showed me that I was heading to an empty place. In this dream, I was over at my Grandpa's house with my sister, a few older cousins, and a few younger cousins. We all decided to go out to the backyard. Then I pulled some bud out of my pocket and began to give some to everyone, even my younger cousins. Then we all smoked our doobies and one of my older cousins put the rest back in my pocket, because I couldn't find my own pocket. Right then, my dad came in and I woke up and I was freaking out because I don't want to be a bad influence on anyone. I saw right there that my life was going nowhere. So I quit doing all drugs. I also realized that without Christ I am nothing. I gave my life to Him. I started to live a new life. I knew once I accepted Christ I would never be the same again, and that scared me, but at the same time I was also filled with joy. So of course, I was all for it!"

Whether it was divine intervention, with Pastor Paul leading the way to salvation, or the power of Christ coming to

Joshua in a dream, to me it was a true miracle. While it might never be possible to save my son from a too-early death, this revelation saved him from destroying whatever time he had left on this earth. Just as I had found strength and peace when I embraced God at a most difficult time in my life, I believed that Joshua was finding the same at this crossroad in his life and that gave me great comfort.

Joshua had always loved music and writing lyrics for songs. One of his special education teachers, who had discovered his passion, gave him a book of rhyming words which inspired him even more. He was a poet at heart and

though he could no longer write, I became his pen as he dictated words to me. We spent many hours, months, and years doing this together. He loved rap music and in the beginning of our musical liaison, his lyrics sometimes shocked me. His words were harsh and sometimes off-color, but I knew he was expressing his own deep-seated pain and disappointment and that this was an important outlet for him to share his emotions. I had to honor him and let him be whoever he needed to be. After he became closer to God, his lyrics softened and he began to write more songs from his heart, words he needed to share, telling everyone that God loves them exactly as they are. From the age of 16 until he was 20, Joshua wrote eight full-length songs that reflected how he saw the world. Auntie Wanda's son Bryan, a music minister at church, helped Joshua and some of his friends record five of them. His words brought great comfort to me as I felt the changes that were lifting his spirit. Joshua hoped that his words would reach around the world and, much later, I was able to help him do that.

From *"This World"*:
"Remember homie this world's filled with hope. You just need to know the place to go, even though I used to smoke dope, God changed my life so now I must learn to cope."

From *"Only Jesus is the Way"*:
"I will stop and pray every single day. No matter what I will say, I hope they will know…only Jesus is the way."

From *"Life After Death"*:
"When life after death is here I know I won't shed one more tear, so tell me when the time is near homie. I have no fear."

Over the years since our divorce, I had remained in good friendship with my first husband Gary and he became a pseudo "uncle" to my children, coming to visit with his daughter Selina every summer. We would also go to Kelowna BC Canada to visit Gary, his parents Grampa George and Gramma Lucille and the family. Joshua and Selina formed a strong bond and deep everlasting love for one another. She became a very important part of his life, someone he felt safe with and who believed in him. She was like a daughter to me

and I cherish the relationship we carry to this day.

My incredible son, who had turned his life away from drugs and towards God, was now forced to deal with yet another, life-changing crisis. He was losing his sight. One day, when we were shopping at the mall, he ran straight into a concrete garbage container and did not seem to notice what was directly in front of him. I found subtle ways to test his sight without saying much about what I had seen. I would sit in a room, without moving or saying a word, waiting to see if he would notice me. He did not. His friend Alex remembered how I held up a finger and asked Joshua how many fingers he could see. I was holding up my middle finger. I knew if he could see what I was doing it would get an honest reaction. He could not see, but we all managed to laugh and make light of the sad truth. I had found a way to defuse the situation and take away some of the seriousness of the moment and that is how it was in our household. He was 18 and would never see me or anything else clearly again. He was diagnosed as legally blind and again my heart broke for him. Joshua never told anyone he was losing his sight and because he had memorized his way around our house and his school, even his friends did not know he had lost most of his vision. He could see shadows and some movement but could not see faces or details. Unless his friends came up to him, he could not even tell they were nearby. This, of course, initially plummeted him into a deep depression, made even worse because he had to rely more on his para-educator to help him navigate the school. It was yet another loss to grieve for both of us.

I kept my tears and sadness to myself and never showed it to him. My purpose in life – to create as much joy as I could for my children – helped me stay focused. Once again I knew how important it was to step toward the problem and educate our friends and others around us about his vision by asking them to address him by name, to speak clearly and more slowly when they talked with him so he could hear and respond. Now his abilities to hear and to speak were compromised as well and people often turned to me to repeat what he had said. I continued to be amazed by Joshua's attitude as his disease stole increasingly more from him.

One day he told his Auntie Wanda that although he couldn't see clearly, he saw an aura of color that changed with each person he was around. When he was frustrated or angry he would turn to his faith for strength and courage, praying and listening to the Bible on tape, memorizing scripture, and listening to Christian music for inspiration.

It has always been important for me to have a sense of purpose and wanting Joshua to have as much purpose in his life as possible, I decided to help him find a job - an important right of passage for any young adult.

I took him to a local theatre to apply for a part-time job. For the next two years, he worked there greeting customers and tearing their tickets. Some of the other theatre employees helped him from time-to-time and were compassionate and supportive in every way possible. My son was not a quitter. Moviegoers often said his smile and cheerful greeting brightened their days.

Joshua, just like his mother, could never sit still. He especially loved his swimming lessons and was extremely happy when his young, adult female instructor would hold him up and challenge him to kick, move his arms and feet, and hold his breath. She was always impressed by how long he could stay under water. Despite all of the things he could no longer do, he remained a big flirt and loved the ladies. When he was introduced to any girl or woman, he always asked them if they were married. It made us all laugh and we would tease him. With all sincerity he would tell the girls how beautiful they looked and I could see how many of them needed to hear that. Some knew he was legally blind and others did not. He just said he saw their true hearts and that is what he responded to.

I had raised him to understand that kindness would carry him throughout his life and that a loving word or smile can mean so much to the person receiving it. Joshua's words not only made these girls happy, it warmed my heart to see the positive effects he had on others. He had absorbed my message and example of caring for others through words and acts of kindness. One of his friends told me Joshua saw the good in everyone. Joshua had a life to live and no time to waste.

By the time both of my children were teenagers we had spoken about life and death enough for them to understand that their disease would possibly – probably – shorten their lives. I told them over the years that no one has guarantees in life and reminded them of some of the people they knew who had passed. Death, I told them, comes to all of us and it is our responsibility to live our best life rather than focus on our inevitable death. I told them many times I had no fear of death, only a fear of living a life without joy, peace, and a sense of purpose. Though I never shared precisely what I knew about the average lifespan for children with Friedrich's Ataxia, they intuitively knew the truth. We all knew and had made an unwritten pact and promised to live each day appreciating the gift it was. I imagine our conversations about such serious things were unique. Most parents are not forced to face a reality where they will likely outlive their children, but this was true for me. Growing up, my family spoke freely about death and often joked about what we wanted from our parents once they died. It was done with humor and in a light manner, but still, it was spoken of and this made it easier for me to talk about it with my children. Knowing what we all knew, we kept going, one day at a time.

Joshua filled his life watching *"Friends"* and other TV comedies, writing lyrics to songs, going to youth group at church, and listening endlessly to music and audio books. He watched Christian-themed movies, had friends over, continued working at the theatre, loved his swimming lessons, and visited Keith mostly every other weekend. At night, when he was home with me, he cherished listening to me read to him, including the entire Harry Potter series, voice intonations included. These were precious moments for both of us and we cherished every minute. Joshua also loved small children and volunteered as a recess helper at the elementary school he once attended. He adored the children, who did not seem to judge him because of his disabilities, kids who would come up and talk with him and share some of their own problems. They seemed to feel safe with him and he loved that. He would encourage them and send them off to play.

Andrew and Tommy were his best friends and all three were addicted to video games, with fantasy games being their favorite. Tommy often pushed Joshua in his manual wheelchair down our street to a small hill, where he would jump on the back of the wheelchair and off they flew, laughing and hollering like a couple of crazy, daredevil teenagers, which is exactly who they were. I sometimes caught them in the garage setting fire to small things, including unsuspecting Star Wars figures, causing some trouble and seeing just how far they could push the envelope. Their antics often tested my patience and nerves and I would scold them, but I was not really angry. In the end I wanted my son to live his best life and find joy wherever he could, even if it drove me a little crazy. Tommy and Andrew never treated Joshua as different, as anyone other than a real friend and they remained close for the remainder of Joshua's life.

"Warhammer," a popular fantasy board game with action figures, was something I also shared with Joshua. I spent hundreds of hours over a two-year period helping him paint Warhammer armies for the game. Because he could no longer see, I would ask what colors he wanted on each piece and follow his very specific directions. I lost some of my own eyesight, straining to get the colors in just the right place, a small price to pay to see the joy in my son's face. At the Games Workshop store, I would put the dice in his hands, watch him toss them, and then tell me or someone else where to move the characters. The shop employees and guests enjoyed Joshua and it thrilled me to see the admiration on their faces. He was resilient and always grateful for anyone's help.

At 20, Joshua's faith and devotion to God grew deeper. He asked me and Jessyca, one of his caregivers, to read the Bible to him and had us highlight the verses meaning the most to him. He told me how he wanted to "walk" in the footsteps of Jesus so I asked Keith if he would be willing to take Joshua to Israel. I knew how much they loved each other, and I saw this as an opportunity for them to have a great adventure together. Both were clean and sober and experiencing renewed hope and faith in their lives. They planned their trip, hired a tour guide, and I did my best trying to let go of the worry I had about Joshua's care and safety. They were gone for three weeks, the most meaningful and remarkable journey of Joshua's life. He was fully dependent on others for his care. They were his eyes, feet, and hands. He was carried in his wheelchair down to the Jordan river to be baptized in the same place as Jesus. He somehow managed to ride a camel in the desert and raved about the delicious food he ate during his entire trip. He floated in the Dead Sea, amazed no one had to hold him up because of the heavy minerals in the water. He journeyed to Bethlehem, where Jesus was born, touched the place of the Lord's birth, and worshipped in Old Jerusalem at the Wailing Wall. I made a scrapbook of his journey and, knowing he was unable to see it, went through it with him, picture-by-picture, describing what was on the page. I could see by the expression of joy on his face he was reliving every moment as he listened to me. When we finished, he said "Mom, I really want us to go there together some day." I told him I would honor his wish. That day came, but not the way he envisioned.

There were plenty of tough moments that felt impossible to handle as Joshua's disease progressed. When I remembered the hurdles we had already cleared, I knew we could conquer anything ahead of us. When I began to feel anxious, I realized I was looking into the future and not staying in the present. When facing a situation that felt insurmountable, I tried to remember I only had to take one step at a time and, by doing that, we would all get through it. This is how I managed to survive to this point. If I had done it up until now, I could do it going forward, one step at a time. The best predictor of future behavior is by looking at our past. I had done well, both for myself and for my children. I was ready to move forward no matter what awaited us.

Journey to Israel

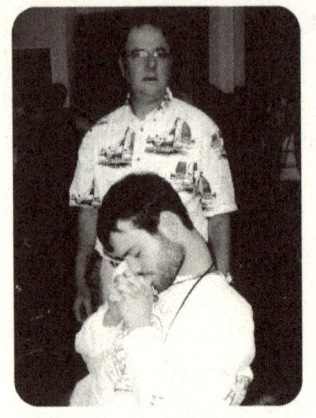

CHAPTER 11

Leah's Journey – Teen Years

"A hero is an ordinary person who finds the strength to persevere and endure in spite of overwhelming obstacles."
—Christopher Reeve

The caregivers I hired over the years helped "normalize" my life in so many ways. They gave me the respite I needed in order to stay strong, healthy and positive. They became friends and confidants to Joshua and Leah and provided many social opportunities that teenagers and young adults need. They handled bathing, dressing and feeding responsibilities and I was always very careful to find young, energetic and positive people who would add fun and joy to our lives. It was important that they fit in with our entire family and not just the kids because we spent so much time together and needed to work together to create a happy life.

Joshua was 16 and Leah was 15 when Tammi, our first beloved caregiver, left us in 2001. She got married, had a baby, and needed to care for her own little family. A blessing in our lives, we were sad to see her go but nonetheless happy for her. I needed to find a new caregiver and once again began the search. It was then that Jessie Graham, a friend from Joshua's church, literally burst into our lives and brought fun and laughter for us all. Her energy kept us moving forward and the kids loved going with her to sports events and church activities. While she wasn't with us for long, she definitely left her mark on our hearts.

Then, in August 2001, Jessyca Swatman came bouncing into our lives and for the next six years helped our family with limitless love, caring, and friendship. The kids met her through friends at an MDA camp and Leah had already formed a deep connection with her. She walked a little on the wild side and was bright, funny, and adventurous. She took Joshua and Leah to parties, escorted them to their proms, accompanied them on dates and, being a very "girlie" girl, helped Leah with her hair and makeup. Jessyca provided every opportunity for my teenagers to do normal things with kids their age. She helped them and, sharing some of the burden of making sure my children found joy in their lives, she helped me too. She was more like a big sister and friend. She told us repeatedly how she looked forward to coming to work, loved our family, and wanted us to adopt her. I may not have agreed with all the choices she made, such as taking Leah to parties and inviting friends over when I was away, but I always knew she had good intentions and an incredible spirit. I trusted her to care for Joshua and Leah when I needed to take care of myself and leave the house for short vacations.

Cliff and I kept seeing each other when we could, but were still not living together. He had proposed a couple of times, and I kept saying "no." I felt he did not really know what he was getting himself into and I never wanted to be torn between my children and another person. The kids and I had settled into a nice and predictable routine and, having upset their lives before, I was reluctant to make any other big changes. Both Joshua and Leah were no longer angry with me and we seemed to have healed from the brokenness. When they were with Keith every other weekend, I was with Cliff and, at least for me, it seemed as if all was well. Cliff, though, was determined to marry me and wanted to be more of a support for us all. When we were together, it was hard to hide my fatigue from my demanding life. I was giving all my energy to my children and often had little left for him.

Being the smart man he was, Cliff asked the children privately if they would be okay if he married me and, surprisingly, they gave an unqualified "yes"! They wanted their mom to be happy and the few times they saw me with Cliff, they were convinced I was. On August 25, 2001, we married in a beautiful, small chapel in Issaquah, Washington. My father and siblings flew in from Canada, and Cliff's mother, two daughters, and grandchildren joined 75 of our friends. It was a happy time, a joyous moment in our challenging lives. My father, in his beautiful tenor voice, sang "Ave Maria" at our wedding, and it would be the last time I heard him sing. We celebrated with an Italian-style reception at my home in Auburn. A most perfect day.

Cliff moved in with me, Joshua, and Leah. There were, inevitably, some difficult moments blending our families, such as Joshua struggling, being torn between Cliff and his allegiance to his father. Cliff, who had been living alone for three years, found it impossible to get a good night's sleep, which was often disrupted by the kids' calling for me. They needed help going to the bathroom and needed to be turned at least twice every night, something they could not do on their own. Cliff, worried about my lack of sleep and fatigue and because he was sleep-deprived, often lost patience when the kids ran into walls with their wheelchairs. Though he knew it was unintentional, Cliff was upset watching the walls get destroyed. His frustrations with my children typically led to "the talk." We never had serious fights about this, but I reminded him I knew coming to live with us would be a lot to take on. I told him I would not be hurt or offended if he wanted to live away from us, though we would remain married. He stayed and, with time, he learned to accept our lives as unusual and challenging. He came to ignore the things that often upset him, and a sense of peace settled in our home.

Fourteen-year-old Leah seemed far more accepting of my divorce from Keith, comfortable with Cliff and strangely complacent about her progressive disease. Her disabilities never seemed to hamper her ability to attract boys. They were always around, wanting to date her.

Her greatest challenge was her disconnect with Keith. She craved his love and attention, but I began to see he thought of her as her mother's daughter. He seemed to transfer his anger at me to Leah. When he was upset with me, it showed up in how he treated her and when she stood up for herself, he shut her down. I questioned Keith about his behavior but he emphatically denied being unnecessarily mean to her. Rather than confront him again, Leah chose to avoid him. Her discomfort with her father presented itself in other ways with her friends. Karla, once inseparable from Leah, grew tired of Leah wanting exclusive rights to her friendship. After a terrible fight, Karla moved on to other girls, leaving Leah behind. Though she made new friends and was well-liked at school, she still felt alone and lonely. When she invited girls over, she often became jealous of their friendships with others and would berate them. Leah hated it when I came into her room when others were there, jealous that my outgoing personality would distract their attention from her. She felt she could not compete and her friends never understood why she seemed jealous of her own mother. She tried to explain this to me, speaking with her compromised hearing and slurred, slow speech, that she could not take part in the conversations if there was more than one person in the room.

Like any mother, I was troubled to see my daughter hurting both physically and emotionally. I wanted to help Leah find things that might give her life purpose, keep her busy, and make her happy.

She had some previous experience with the "Dream On" pageant and went to an audition for a local modeling agency.

Leah was accepted into their training program and partici-pated in several events, including a runway modeling show. She was the only model in a wheelchair and was incredibly nervous, but the other girls were friendly and helped her feel comfortable. I saw her confidence and self-esteem grow as she told her family and friends about her modeling experiences. She was asked to do several photo shoots, both alone and with other girls, and the photos were featured in several national education-focused publications and in various stores around the country including Goodwill.

With her newfound confidence, we volunteered at Muscu-lar Dystrophy events and met many new friends in that community. At 16, she was approached by MDA and asked to be the Goodwill Ambassador for the State of Washington. She was deeply honored and accepted the invitation. Required to speak at events, promote MDA camps, and support their fundraising efforts, Leah loved every minute of it. She truly loved inspiring other people and stated that though people considered her shy, once they got to know her, she was friendly and outgoing.

Following her brother's lead to find purpose, Leah volun-teered as a reading tutor at the local elementary school and helped with recess. She was able to stay in regular classes at her high school and managed to take jewelry-making classes and learn sign language. She was a very pretty girl with a beautiful smile and a succession of boyfriends from elemen-tary school until her life's end. As she got older, I worried she might get pregnant, either intentionally or by accident. I knew, because of her disabilities, she would never be able to protect herself from an assault. She was vulnerable. When she was 16, I told her I wanted to protect her by putting her on Depo-Provera shots to prevent pregnancy. She understood and agreed at that time although later it would become a point of contention.

What Leah wanted more than anything else was time...

one-on-one with me or with any of her friends. Time was her love language. She saw the time I spent with Joshua, attending to his hobbies to keep him interested in doing different things.

Auntie Nadine

I needed to find a way to give her special time as well. In the summer, I took her on road trips to Canada to visit my family. She loved being alone in the car with me as we traveled to see her grandparents, my former in-laws, and my first husband Gary and his family. I was all hers for the 17-hour drive. She would listen to pop and country music on the radio and often demand I quit singing along. She often said: "Mom, stop... you're ruining the song." We laughed about that and I just kept singing. In contrast, Joshua would say "mom... keep singing, I love your voice."

We sometimes talked about what Leah wanted to do with her life and dreams about her future, though unlike her outgoing brother, Leah was more of an introvert, content with the quiet times and happy being alone with me. She was unable to move much on her own and needed full care when she would eat, go to the bathroom, or bathe. During our adventures, I often had to bring a portable potty to accommodate her. At 18 and fully grown, she was difficult to lift and sometimes I had to ask for help from strangers. Most of the time, though, I managed to do it alone, which she preferred, and it made me physically stronger. Once again, I would vow to show acts of kindness to strangers whenever I saw a need that I could help with. There were brief moments when extreme fatigue overwhelmed me and I wondered how long I could keep doing this with Leah, but I always knew I would never give up. If my children could endure what they were dealing with, so could I.

Although there was always a possibility that one of the kids would get sick or something would happen requiring us  to change plans, I was on a mission to give them every opportunity possible. This meant making plans and shifting them if necessary. I would not be led by fear and more often than not, our plans were achieved. Occasionally, I took Leah with me on my Pampered Chef incentive trips, rewards based on my performance. This first was a trip to Disneyworld in Florida. It was my first plane ride alone with her, without family, friends or caregivers to help me. For one of the only times I can remember, I felt very anxious from the moment we got on the plane and by the time we arrived in Florida, my anxiety only got worse. I was alone with Leah, who was still getting used to her new wheelchair and the tasks of figuring out transportation, bathing her, and navigating through the park and all of the Disney rides overwhelmed me.

The only thing Leah felt was excitement. We arrived at the park, tickets in hand, but once we got inside, I froze. I looked one way, then another, but could not get my bearings. I knew *where* I wanted to go but had no idea how to get there. I felt my heart pounding and breathing became shallow and quick. My chest felt tight and I felt as if my head would explode. I was terrified, standing behind her chair, pretending to push her. I quietly began to cry, tears streaming down my face. With everything I had been through – all the trials, doctor's appointments, surgeries for my children, and the chaos of a failed marriage – I had never really collapsed until that moment.

Leah kept saying "Let's go Mom," but I had no idea where to go or how to get there. I had never experienced a full-blown panic attack, but in the middle of Disneyworld, I had one. We wandered around the park but returned to our hotel fairly quickly. We still had two more days and although I managed to settle-down a bit, the anxiety lingered for the entire time. The moment I got home, I crashed for two full days. That panic was the most terrifying and debilitating experience of my life and, thankfully, it never happened again. Remembering that moment, I think I was completely overwhelmed, having no control in a new and strange environment and no one to turn to for help. I had to manage everything—something I was able to do in my own, familiar places—but here, in a different world, I unraveled. Alone, exhausted, and scared. I should have planned less activities and more rest time for us both but at that time I was laser focused on giving Leah every opportunity to experience all that Disneyworld had to offer. In the end we were both overly exhausted.

After the near-debacle at Disneyworld, we came home and life returned to normal, such as it was. Leah, always wanting to help people, volunteered to take part in a drug trial at the National Institute of Health in Virginia. The hospital was testing new medication meant to deter the progression of the thickening of heart muscle. Leah was eager to participate. For her it was another adventure, a way to change the mundane parts of her life. The testing was neither complicated nor invasive. She stayed in the hospital for three nights, was given a medication several times a day, and asked about any symptoms she might be having. It gave her a sense of purpose, a way to help find treatments for FA. Every year we traveled around the country to various Ataxia conferences. She loved hanging out with the other young girls she met who also had FA.

In these environments, her true personality flourished and she formed some very special friendships, especially with a young man coincidentally named Keith. She was 16 and more than ready to have a more serious boyfriend. Keith, like Leah,

had FA and was also in a wheelchair. Several times over the ensuing years Keith and his brother or a caregiver would fly from their home in Virginia to visit us, and Leah and I also visited him in his hometown. Keith and Leah spoke on the phone regularly and got matching tattoos symbolizing their friendship and love for one other. They were dragonfly tattoos, which had always been Leah's symbol for courage and dignity, something she had read about previously.

Keith's stepfather, Ron, became the founding president of FARA – the Friedreich's Ataxia Research Alliance – dedicated to bringing scientists from around the world together to collaborate and share their data in hope of finding treatments and a cure for FA. After they had known each other for close to eight years, meeting at conferences, visiting each others homes and speaking on the phone, Leah spoke to Keith for the last time. With just hours to live, he wanted to hear her voice before he passed. They exchanged only a few words and mostly cried with one another, but were truly comforted by those final moments together.

In 2003, Leah was now 16 and, just as Joshua had received a wish from the Make-a-Wish Foundation, it was her turn. Leah had decided to wait for her wish until she was a bit older and could pick something extra special. Jessyca, our creative caregiver, came up with an amazing idea: let Leah take part in the People's Teen Choice Awards on National TV. This is a special awards ceremony where teens get to honor and vote for the year's biggest achievements in music, film, sports, television, fashion, social media. Leah thought that was about the most fabulous thing she could ask for. I contacted the Foundation and they did not hesitate for a moment. The two wish-granters, Jill and Sue, arrived at our home, brought small gifts for both children, and began asking Leah what she envisioned for her trip to Los Angeles. Not one to shy away, not this time, Leah said she wanted to present Kelly Clarkson, that year's winner of American Idol, with her big award and she wanted her cousin Heidi to come with her. On August 4, 2003, we arrived at the Alaska Airlines gate, greeted by balloons and signs. As we boarded the plane, the pilot announced they had an extra-special guest on board, Leah Chalcraft, who was having her wish granted by the Make-a-Wish Foundation. Everyone applauded my very happy girl.

In Los Angeles, we were greeted by other Foundation representatives, escorted to a wheelchair-accessible van and taken to our hotel near Universal Studios. We had full access to a driver who took us wherever we wanted to go. After a much-needed rest, we headed to Rodeo Drive. Leah had heard about this fancy place in movies, but wanted to see if for herself. We went into Tiffany's and imagining she was Julia Roberts in *"Pretty Woman,"* she bought a small charm with an "L" on it to symbolize that special moment. She wanted to get her nose pierced and she and Heidi wanted to get tattoos. I could not deny her anything at that point and had decided long ago to do my utmost to make her wishes come true. She had the word "Love" – in Japanese Kanji writing – tattooed on the underside of her wrist.

The day before the People's Teen Choice Awards show, we were taken to the venue for a dress rehearsal and to meet David Spade, the emcee. Leah was low on energy after the plane trip and our excursion to Rodeo Drive and was nervous about her upcoming performance. She was tired and needed rest. David was gracious and after a bit of joking and going through what she would have to do the next day, we went back to the hotel to basically collapse. The next morning, the day of the big event, two makeup and hair artists arrived at our hotel and pampered Leah, treating her as they would a superstar.

We dressed to match the award show's "beach" theme and were off to the studio. We were greeted at the venue by reporters and paparazzi as I pushed Leah's wheelchair down the blue carpet. Ryan Seacrest of *American Idol* stopped and asked Leah questions as if he was talking to a movie star: "Who is your favorite pop singer?" and "How much fun are you having?" As we waited in a small courtyard at the end of the blue carpet, other real celebrities ended up near us. We met Jimmy Kimmel, Tony Hawk, Ashton Kutcher, Adam Sandler, Jessica Alba, Britney Spears, and so many other famous folks. They all stopped to greet us, sign autographs, and pose with Leah for pictures. Leah was in heaven and I was too. I was thrilled for her and it was exciting meeting people I had only seen on television or in movies. Sitting in the green room, waiting to go on stage, we spent almost an hour talking with Paula Abdul. Leah was nervous, excited, a little overwhelmed, but thrilled beyond words. When it was time to present the awards, I was worried Leah would not be able to read her remarks from a large cue card on a teleprompter. Her moment came as they wheeled her onto the stage. Alongside two other Make-a-Wish kids and figure-skating champion Tara Lapinski, they announced Kelly Clarkson as winner of the 2003 People's Teen Choice Award for new music artists. Leah beamed as Kelly came out and graciously accepted her large, surfboard award. I was thrilled for them both.

Over the next few years, besides losing her ability to walk and use her hands, Leah's vision, hearing, and energy levels gradually diminished. She had met a couple of service dog puppies at an MDA camp and decided she wanted her own.

People's Teen Choice Awards 2003 w/ Kelly Clarkson

She was 18, about to graduate from high school, and thought the companionship of a dog would be both helpful and comforting. We spent two weeks at the Summit Assistance Dog program in Anacortes, about two hours north of Seattle. After only a couple of introductions to various dogs, Leah bonded almost immediately to Bella, a beautiful two-year-old Golden Retriever. After a command to get up on Leah's lap, it was love at first sight. Over two weeks of training, Leah

learned how to manage Bella with very specific commands. At home, Bella was fully trained and entirely amazing. She could turn lights on and off, open doors (including handicapped-accessible ones), pick up a dropped pencil, and retrieve anything Leah might need. She went with Leah everywhere, to school or shopping at the mall. Bella made it easier for people to approach Leah. They first saw the dog and not the wheelchair. Though Bella wore a patch saying, "I'm working, please don't pet me," sometimes people would forget and found the big, beautiful dog irresistible. The rationale behind the vest was to prevent Bella from being distracted and keep her focus on Leah. After having a few paws run over by Leah's wheelchair, Bella learned to keep a short distance from the wheels, though she was always tied to the chair. Leah learned what commands to give and Bella learned what they meant. They became inseparable. Bella made Leah's life happier and, in one shocking moment, saved her life.

During a terrible, very windy storm, a tree fell on our home and we were forced to move into a hotel for several months while repairs were made. I found a place with two bedrooms on the bottom floor with a door opening to a long walking and biking path just outside. On one side of the path was a steep ravine, filled with big, beautiful evergreen trees cascading down the slope, leading to a rapidly flowing river. Leah decided to take Bella for a walk and as they left I noticed Bella was not tied to the wheelchair. They had been together long enough and we knew Bella would not leave Leah's side even if she was loose. I began to worry when they did not return after 30 minutes and as I was about to go out to look for them, there was a knock at the hotel door. It was a firefighter asking if I had a daughter named Leah who was in a wheelchair. My heart stopped as a million scenarios ran through my head. Had she been hit by a car? Did Bella run off and get hit? I tried not to imagine the worst as I followed the firefighter a short way down the path. With her vision getting worse, Leah had not noticed the edge of the path. She maneuvered her chair too far over and the power wheelchair tumbled over the edge and began sliding down the ravine towards the water. The accident happened in a mostly clear spot, with few trees to stop her downward slide. She eventually hit a tree and came to a stop about one foot from the water's edge.

Only by the grace of God, Bella was not tethered to the chair and her leash fell from Leah's grip. Bella sat below with her for a few minutes, licking her face, then ran back up to the path and sat there, looking down until someone noticed and called her over. Bella would not move from her spot. She sat there, watching over Leah until someone came to her. A man rushed to see what was going on, thinking it odd that this dog was just sitting there, glancing down at the river. He saw Leah on her side, strapped into her wheelchair, unable to move. After calling 911, within minutes the fire department came to the rescue. Leah was in shock, but able to give her name. With that information, the firefighter came to the hotel, asked which room we were in, and gave us the shocking news. At the scene, the firefighters decided it was safer not to move her out of her wheelchair, but to turn it upright and pull her up the hill while she was still in it. They were concerned she might have broken bones and possibly her neck. She had scrapes and scratches on her hands and face and then immediately took her and Bella to Valley Medical Center for X-rays and checked Bella for any injuries. Leah had scratches on her face and complained her leg hurt.

Cliff stayed with Joshua as Keith and I rushed to the hospital. I cried the whole way there. I sobbed, thinking about my baby who had already faced so many challenges in her life. Looking at my daughter, in shock and mortified by the accident, all I could do was hold her close and tell her she would be okay. Leah remembered most of what happened and told me she tried to yell a command to Bella but did not have enough air in her lungs to shout. She just lay there, imagining the worst. Would anyone ever find her? Bella, her smart, trusting, and ever-loyal companion, made sure someone did. Leah did, in fact, have a broken leg, but she healed well and quickly. The whole frightening episode played over-and-over in my mind in the months ahead, but it was a story Leah told with great pride, how Bella the wonder dog saved her life.

Volunteering and finding ways to help others became Leah's passion and she offered her services at the local YMCA front desk, greeting guests and checking them in. She loved people and the older she got, the more outgoing she became. With her love of music, she applied for a summer job scanning tickets at the nearby White River Amphitheater. I knew she would not be able to handle the job alone, so I applied too and was hired as a supervisor at the VIP tent and was able to help Leah when she needed to use the bathroom. Though it was difficult for her to use the scanning guns, she made it through the summer. She loved seeing the concerts for free, in particular watching Kelly Clarkson, whom she had presented with her Teen Choice award a few years earlier. She loved making her own money and the feeling of independence having a job.

In 2007, when Joshua was 22 and Leah was 21, their caregiver, Jessyca, had to leave us and once again we faced the challenge of finding someone new. We needed someone who was strong enough to lift and transfer my adult children and committed to helping them enrich their lives socially. I checked with families and friends we knew through the Muscular Dystrophy Association and were quickly introduced to Brianne Sembar, a friend of a friend. Leah already knew "Bre" from previous MDA events and liked her. Bre, a 26 year old spirited young woman, was nervous when we first met since she had never been a caregiver, but her smile and positive attitude convinced me she would be a great fit for us all. Joshua and Leah were happy to have another caregiver in their lives, especially someone who was a young, fun, quirky, and energetic person that would hopefully stay with them for the remainder of their lives. In a very short time Bre became part of our family and like another daughter to Cliff and I.

In her final year of high school, Leah began dating Jason, a bright, handsome young man. Cliff and I liked him immediately. We saw how much he cared for Leah and ignored his occasional clumsiness. Jason was pleasant to be around and made Leah happy, which was always the most important thing to us. He helped her experience everything all the other students were experiencing and was willing to do whatever it took to make her senior year a happy one. After graduation, we saw more potential in him than he saw for himself and pushed him to apply for grants so he could attend Renton Technical College.

Cliff and I agreed to allow Jason to live with Leah in her room, set up like a small apartment. Keith was completely against the idea on moral grounds, but I wanted Leah to live as many other girls her age were, with the right to make decisions for themselves. It is another right of passage. I wanted to give her the gift of making choices whenever possible and to control as much as she could. I recognized that she was living a life where the norm was more about giving up control. Though this decision might be seen by some as risky and even inappropriate, it was what my daughter wanted. Many of her friends were leaving home and heading to college or to new jobs. Leah would never be able to do those things on her own and always have to live at home. Having Jason move in with her was the only way she might ever be able to know what it was like to live with someone she loved, in a true partnership.

They both registered for school at Renton Technical College, Leah in the para-educator program so she could learn to help kids with special needs and Jason entered the IT program. He awakened her every morning, dressed her, and helped feed her when they came for breakfast. Together with Bella, they were picked up every day by a wheelchair-accessible bus, then returned home at the end of the day. Jason helped her with her bathroom needs at school and shared lunch with her every day. For the next 18 months, they were together, but for reasons I never understood, Leah suddenly asked him to move out. I never learned why she did this, but I never regretted our decision to have Jason with us. I knew how important these relationships were for her. And though they remained friends, I never questioned her choices. I had to give her the freedom to do whatever she needed to do for the rest of her life, at least most of the time.

When she was 20, Leah told us how badly she wanted a baby. Though she did not have a boyfriend, she thought having a child was a rite of passage she was entitled to have. She begged me to stop the Depo-Provera shots, started years earlier, and allow her to get pregnant. I refused. Although I had rarely taken any decision about their lives from them, this one was non-negotiable. I was still caring for my own children and, with the likelihood I would outlive them, I did not want another child. I had raised two children in the most arduous and difficult circumstances imaginable. I could not imagine going through this again. I understood her desire, but that was the one and only thing I could not allow to happen. That was one thing I could control, but I had no power to prevent what was coming.

The idea we can control every element of our lives is a deeply held belief by many and completely unachievable. I was one who believed that and it only led to anxiety and eventually a panic attack. I had to learn to let go of that notion forever, to stop worrying about the small things and keep my focus on the big picture, to hold fast to my vision of helping my children find purpose in their lives. I could not change what was happening to my children, only control my attitude and try to be a model of positivity for them. Though it sometimes seemed easier to surrender and fall into darkness, I chose – against all odds – to stay in the light.

Leah with cousins Sarah, Rachel and Ariane Bolivar

CHAPTER 12

Losing Joshua

"When someone is going through a rough time... just sit with them. No preaching, no advice. Just be there."
—anonymous

Joshua was 22 when he choked on a piece of chicken and had to be rushed by ambulance to the hospital. His airway was partially blocked and he struggled to breathe. The emergency medical technician told me he was optimistic because Joshua was able to take in a small amount of oxygen, but I was terrified watching every shallow breath as my precious son's lips turned blue. All I could think about was whether this would be the last time I would see my son alive. Any parent witnessing their child carried away in an ambulance would be frightened, but in my case, I thought with all his physical challenges, choking on a piece of chicken might be the thing that finally ended his life. I had never thought this way before, allowing the possibility of imminent death to enter our lives in any dramatic way. I always managed to overcome each obstacle and move forward, pushing aside the possibility of my children's lives ending. Perhaps I knew, with a mother's intuition, that the end, if not in that moment of choking, was near.

I called Keith, told him what was happening and to meet me at the hospital. Within an hour, the doctor came out and told us Joshua would be fine and the large piece of chicken had been successfully removed from his esophagus. Now I could breathe easier too, with a deep sense of relief, as I watched my frail, little boy lying in his hospital bed. When he saw me and his father, Joshua began to cry, something I had rarely seen him do. He told us he had seen angels watching over him during his surgery and fully believed he would never have a chance to see us again. He expected to die that day, but God had other plans.

Joshua, now 22, was weak and frail and had little energy for physical activities. His health was declining and he spent most of his days in bed, listening to music and books on tape, watching movies, and hearing the Bible read to him. He loved having us read and help him memorize his favorite verses, which gave him hope. One he particularly loved was: "For I know the plans I have for you, says the Lord. They are plans for good and not disaster, to give you a future and a hope" (Jeremiah 29.11). He had miraculously turned his life around and my concern for his safety from drugs and alcohol was no longer an issue. He was at peace with the choices he made and found purpose in sharing his faith and belief in God's love for everyone.

I, on the other hand, was not at peace. As both Joshua's and Leah's health continued to decline, I became more and more anxious, wondering if today would be the day I would lose my children. I wanted to believe I could control the inevitable outcome of their disease but knew – now more than ever before – that I could not. When they caught a cold, I worried this would be the final blow, the thing that would take their lives. When they were particularly tired and had to spend their days sleeping, I wondered if they would ever have the strength to get out of bed again.

The horror of my children's pending deaths was made worse by the death of my father, a man I deeply loved, who had long ago inspired me with words that shaped so much of my life and my children's lives. In the spring of 2008, he was diagnosed with colon cancer and Cliff and I traveled to Ottawa to see him. In August, we got the call he was dying and I traveled home alone. My heart broke seeing him so weak in his hospital bed, barely able to speak. I lay down next to him and told him I had made something for him, a scrapbook to commemorate his life. I shared each page with him, from his birth to the last picture I had of him. As I closed the book he looked up at me and with great effort said, "LouLou, I'm going to take this to heaven with me." Early the next morning, we got a call that my Dad passed away peacefully. He was 78, a rock in my life.

Death, in its dark and frightening way, now seemed the currency of my life and I needed help. In almost two decades of grappling with my children's illnesses, I had managed to be brave and optimistic, and find a way to help my children find their purpose in life while creating moments of joy for them. Now I was unraveling, feeling my emotional strength draining from me in the wake of my father's death, and watching Joshua and Leah dying before my eyes. I contacted my counselor, Cece, and was able to immediately share all of my fears and worries with her. I was living in a state of abject terror, overly preparing every day for the unimaginable sadness that was my future. Cece helped me regain my balance and belief that I could handle whatever was coming my way. She gave me permission I had never given myself to feel helpless and vulnerable and to sometimes sit alone and cry. She helped me create a space to let myself feel all the sadness I had kept inside, sadness I had been carrying around for many, many years and managed to keep at bay. I was also able to share my frustrations about mine and my kids relationship with Keith and my anxiety about what the future would bring. I needed a safe place to express myself honestly and openly and she provided that.

Even with Joshua's disease progressing at a rapid pace, I

tried not to bring either him or Leah to the doctors more than was necessary. They had been to enough doctors for several lifetimes and hospitalized for more surgeries than any child should have to endure and they hated it. I noticed Joshua was choking more when he ate and had no choice but to take him to the hospital for a very uncomfortable upper GI test. They determined he was a "silent aspirator," meaning he would inhale fluid and food particles into his lungs but his body would not automatically allow him to cough it up. The substances would nest in his lungs, which could cause serious health issues. The doctors said all I could do was to add thickening agents such as gelatin to his liquids, urge him to use a straw, and remind him to chew a lot.

On one cold, winter evening I noticed he was having a difficult time breathing and running a fever. After three days of hovering over him and worrying, I decided I needed to take him back to the doctor. Joshua had pneumonia in one lung and was immediately admitted to the hospital, where he was hydrated and given antibiotics. Five days there seemed like an eternity to him and he desperately wanted to come home. He was finally released into the care of his two mothers, his worried sister and me. Leah hovered over him day and night, watching TV with him, gossiping about their friends. Though he occasionally got annoyed with her, he secretly loved and appreciated her company.

After only a week at home, Joshua ended up back in the hospital, this time with double pneumonia, something the doctors said would be a recurring problem. Joshua's lungs were failing and after still more tests, we were told his heart was getting weaker and other organs were also beginning to fail. In the silence of the waiting room Keith and I held on to each other, crying. No matter what our past history had been, we now shared a frightening and dark reality. Our beautiful, young son was not going to recover and we had to make some very difficult decisions about what to do with the time he had left.

We shared the truth with Joshua about what the doctor told us, but it seemed as if he already knew. The only thing he said to us was, "I just want to go home and never see a hospital or a doctor again." He was done and seemed at peace with his decision. We spoke with the physician who then sent us to talk with the hospital social worker about the ramifications of Joshua's words. She went to speak with Joshua and began asking questions. Did he understand the implications of the choice he was making? What if he got sick again? Would he want to get better? What if the only way to recover was to return to the hospital? He told her he would want to recover, but never wanted to return to the hospital for any reason... ever. She looked at us, looked back at him, and recommended we arrange immediate hospice care for him. This would help him and give us support we would need to care for him for whatever time remained.

For the first time in 16 years, I knew this was the beginning of the end for my dear son. My heart broke listening to him share what he really wanted, to be free from the constraints of medical procedures, diagnoses, tubes, needles, and doctors. I had always allowed him control over his life, fall or fail, without trying to save him. Inside my head I was screaming and begging him not to give up, but I had to quiet my thoughts, let him make this choice, and maintain his dignity in any way he could. He was 22 and of sound mind, even though his ravaged body was failing him. With more strength and courage than I had ever seen in anyone, Joshua was ready to let go and as much as I wanted to, I could neither stop nor save him.

We had spoken of death over the years, but in very general terms. I had told both of my children the only real truth I knew, that everyone is going to die, that only God knows when our time will come or how we would go, so we had to keep living our best life every day. I knew they would die young from this terrible disease, but I tried to keep my focus on living, not on dying. Still, I wanted and needed to know what their wishes were. I knew it was time to talk openly with them both together, finding comfort in each other's words and ideas. This was not all spoken in one single conversation but in several talks over a few months. I knew I would not forget their wishes and encouraged them to speak by asking questions and starting with what I hoped for when my time came. I had grown beyond the limiting strategy of denial and into someone who had moved toward what was hard with courage and openness and truth. I had changed. Even when I wanted to hide and deny and push against reality and my deep sadness, I was learning to embrace what was true and endure the hard feelings and the hard conversations. I told them I wanted to be cremated and have my ashes sprinkled in the ocean because I loved the water and felt so peaceful when I was swimming. I also wanted a certain song, "Footprints in the Sand" by Leona Lewis played at my memorial and hoped people would remember good things about me. I wanted to donate my body for medical research in any way it might be useful. I shared these thoughts with them at different times when we were together to open the conversation so they could tell me what they envisioned for themselves. They wanted their bodies donated for medical research in the hopes of finding a cure for FA and later wanted their bodies cremated and ashes spread. They picked their own favorite songs to be played at their memorial services. Joshua wanted the song "I Will Rise" by Chris Tomlin and Leah wanted "I Hope You'll Dance" by Lee Ann Womack.

We talked easily about these things in an almost light-hearted way, but I think my decision to be open with them took some of their fear away. We shared what each one of us believed about what happens after we die, and what life might look like on the other side. They both believed in God and were certain He had a beautiful place waiting for them. They imagined they would be able to walk again, run freely, and live a life after death without sorrow, pain, or doctors. This was their idea of Heaven and it made me happy to hear their words. They seemed to have no anxiety or fear of dying, but as their mother, I had enough for all of us...an overwhelming unease of how I would be able to handle their passing and how I would find the strength to face the days ahead without them.

With Joshua now 23 and in hospice care at home and using an oxygen tank when he was in bed, the only thing I could control was planning and preparing for his inevitable end. I contacted FARA (Friedreich's Ataxia Research Alliance) and they gave me the information I needed to ensure when the end came, the arrangements for Joshua's body to be donated for research would be in place. I contacted the local neurologist who made sure Joshua's organs would be removed and transported to New York for medical research and I met with the pastor of a local church to plan the details for his memorial service. I arranged for the cremation of his body once the organs were removed. I tried to imagine every detail that I *could* control as I surrendered to the truth I could not save him. It may seem strange I did all of this as my son lay dying, but it was somehow my own way of loving him, ensuring he would be honored after his death, because I knew I would not be organized in the wake of his passing. As the oxygen tanks and medical supplies kept him breathing and living, I attended to the preparations for his dying. It was the most painful, agonizing task of my lifetime. I was trying to prepare for a moment I hoped would be a long time coming, but knew he had only days to live.

One reliable and comforting thing in our lives was the weekly visits from the hospice nurse who came, armed with a smile, to check on Joshua and make sure we had everything we needed to care for him. On one visit I mentioned Joshua had been in her care for seven months and seemed to be doing pretty well. He was able to get out of bed more and go outside on rare occasions. I suggested we might take him off hospice care, but in a very soft, sweet but still firm voice she told me "no." She said the slight surge in energy he was experiencing, called rallying, was common in people preparing for their final days. Just as I was building my capacity to not go into denial and push away reality—I had relapses. This was one of those times when I couldn't accept the truth of her words. Denial was something that protected me in this moment from having to take in something that was just too painful and overwhelming. Denial is not always a bad thing and had served me well over the years. In this moment, I was incapable of hearing what she was telling me. I chose not to listen. My optimistic mind decided this was not going to happen to my son anytime soon. Over the course of my 52 years, I was an expert at denying and pushing away any darkness or pain hovering around me. *"Pick yourself up, brush it off, and just go on."* Echoes from my childhood. My mind might have known the truth, but my heart refused to listen.

On January 31st while Cliff and I were out to dinner and Bre, our caregiver, was home with the children, Keith showed up for a visit. By his own choice, he hadn't seen them for a full month and had barely spoken to them during that time. He was gone by the time we arrived home. Both Joshua and Leah were happy to see him and seemed not to hold grudges against their father.

It is interesting how often primary caregivers get the brunt of anger and resentment and ungratefulness shown to them and those who are not around much get only forgiveness and kindness and gratitude shown to them. My theory is that Joshua and Leah knew without a doubt that I would never abandon them nor would I ever deprive them of my love and devotion, no matter what. It was exhausting for them to always have to show gratitude because their needs were many and they depended on others for every single need in their life. I was a safe place for them to vent and emote and share their frustrations without fear of me walking away. On the other hand, they had to show appreciation and gratitude to others for fear that they would walk away because they couldn't trust the level of commitment from them. I've seen this same truth revealed so many times over the years with the many losses I've experienced. In an odd sort of way, it's a compliment to the ones who are dealing with the challenging and often rebellious emotions of the sick.

When I went into Joshua's bedroom to spend some quiet time with him alone, he looked at me with deep sadness in his eyes and told me he did not know if he would ever see his dad again. I held him close as he cried and I tried to reassure him. I felt his heart beating rapidly and his breathing seemed strained so I laid him back down, gently put the covers over his frail body, and told him just to try and relax. I then went to see Leah who had little to say about her visit with her father other than she was done having expectations about him. She was only sad for her brother, more concerned about him than anyone else.

While I was lying with Leah in her bed, rubbing her back and talking with her, Joshua began screaming in pain. I rushed to his room where he was lying in bed, holding his chest and yelling that his heart hurt. I was frantic. Within just a moment, he began throwing up again and again and wailing in pain, clutching his chest. I rolled him onto his side and held onto him, trying to comfort him, telling him he would be okay although even I did not believe what I was saying. I was terrified and prayed silently for this horrible and frightening moment to pass. Cliff went into Leah's room and tried to comfort her as I yelled for him to bring me my phone. I called the hospice nurse who told me to immediately open the comfort kit of medications they had given me for a moment like this. She said to give him morphine orally and instructed me to slowly increase the dose over the next hour. As Joshua screamed in pain, I gently lifted him into his wheelchair so I could clean his bed and wash him. I then lifted him back into his bed and laid down next to him, holding him in my arms for over an hour as the drugs slowly released him from his suffering.

He was now in a drug-induced coma, but at least he was no longer in pain. As he slept, I went to Leah and held her through her tears. She was suffering too, watching her beloved brother slip away in front of her eyes and seeing her own future staring at her. If she was frightened, she never showed her fear and, in that moment, was only thinking of him, as she always did.

I spent that night in and out of Joshua's bedroom, crying on Cliff's strong shoulders and trying to comfort my boy, hoping he could feel my presence and possibly hear my words. I told him what an honor it was to have been his mother and spoke of other things...talking about everything and nothing... just words to fill the dark and too-quiet space. I continued to administer morphine every half hour as the nurse had instructed and tried to rest in between. The nurse told me to prepare for the worst so I called Keith and told him to come over in the morning. I also called some of Joshua's closest friends and opened our home to all of them the next morning.

The nurse arrived first, then Keith came around 8:30 am and she told us Joshua had only hours to live. I still wanted to believe he would, by some miracle, wake up and be well again. I asked her if there was any chance that might happen and, in her effort to comfort me, she said miracles do happen and there was a slight chance he could. I clung to those words, "slight chance." Why not my son, I thought! He has always been extraordinary, a survivor who has overcome so many challenges in his young life. Perhaps he could even cheat death. There is a fine line between denial and hoping for miracles. Hope can give you a reason to keep going through the unendurable and denial is pretending it isn't happening. In that moment, I wish she would not have tried to give me hope because I got lost in it instead of being completely present with my son as he passed on from this life. I became consumed with imagining impossible things until hours later the nurse snapped me back into reality. "You must keep giving him the morphine because if he does awaken, he will be in terrible pain. His heart is failing."

My son would never wake up again.

A few friends and family then came to the house to say goodbye. I made sure Joshua was never alone in those hours. Bre and a friend, Angie, sat with Joshua as he slept, reading the many Bible verses he had highlighted over the years. I played soft music in his room and found it comforting to have loved ones around him and me. One of Joshua's best friends, Alex, recently told me why he could not be there. He believed if he did not show up, nothing bad would happen. It was Super Bowl Sunday and Alex believed if he just watched the game as was planned everything would be okay. Joshua would be fine and life would go on uninterrupted. "If I don't see it," he told himself, "it will not happen."

But it did.

As I laid next to my son, I whispered in his ear that I loved him so very much and it was okay for him to let go. I told him I would take care of his sister and we would all be fine. He did not need to hold on for us. I knew he would be watching over us with all of the other angels. At 4:45 in the afternoon, Joshua began taking fewer breaths and Bre called me into his room. Keith and Leah followed as we watched and listened, barely breathing ourselves. At 4:54 on February 1, 2008, Joshua James Chalcraft took his final breath. Nothing and no one could have prepared me for that dreadful moment. My heart seemed to stop beating too as I held onto my son, desperately hoping he would take another breath, but it never came. I walked into the living room where our loved ones were waiting. All I wanted to do was crawl into a hole and die with my son. I just stood there, numb, empty, and crushed. Not seeking or wanting comfort from anyone, I wanted to scream at the injustice and cruelty of it all but could not. I had a daughter who needed me now more than ever. Leah and I held on tight to each other and wept. When the tears subsided just a little, she went in alone to say goodbye to her beloved brother. Then it was my turn.

I held my lifeless son in my arms and told him again what an honor it was to have been his mother and what an incredible son he had been. I told him I would not have traded him for a second and I would do it all over again just to have more time with him...despite the struggles and all of the obstacles we faced in his too-short life. Yes, I would do it again. I sat with him in the darkness, kissing him and praying for more time until I was forced to let him go. Two men arrived from the funeral home to take him away. Time was of the essence since his body was going to the University of Washington for organ donation preparations.

Soon everyone was gone and the house was eerily, hauntingly quiet. I put Leah to bed and laid with her until she fell asleep. Then I went into Joshua's room as I had done so many thousands of times to say goodnight, but saw only his empty bed and all of the medical equipment invading his space. I laid in his bed, inhaling his scent from the pillow, and felt a compelling need to get all of the medical paraphernalia out of his room. I called Cliff and said emphatically I wanted the hospital bed, oxygen equipment, and bi-pap machines gone by morning. I wanted his regular bed returned so I could only have the memory of my son without the reminders of his disease. I wanted him back, but I could not have him ever again. The only comfort I felt in that agonizing moment was he was neither suffering nor in pain any longer. It was the only thought I had running through my mind that helped keep me sane in the following months. It was the only thing that gave me even the slightest sense of peace.

The days after Joshua's death are hazy now in my memory, something of a blur for which I am grateful. To reflect back on

LOUISE FRANK

the day he died instantly triggers a pain that has never truly healed. I was going through the motions of living, but not really feeling alive. Part of my soul died with him. I was glad I had prearranged the details of his memorial and a video of his life had been prepared ahead. My favorite pictures of him were ready to be displayed by the urn containing his ashes and the prayer shawl he brought back from Israel was ready to be placed on top of the urn. I called my family in Canada to tell them of Joshua's passing and asked Bre to help Leah contact any of their mutual friends to share information about the memorial service, to be held in two weeks.

I managed to numb myself by focusing on the preparations, trying to make certain everything would be perfect, which helped lessen the searing pain of my devastating loss. I was laser-focused on honoring Joshua by giving him the most personal and meaningful memorial service possible.

The emotional armor I had constructed inside myself finally cracked when I walked into the auditorium of the church and saw 600 people filling the room. Seeing people from all parts of our lives, all touched by Joshua in different ways, overwhelmed me and brought me to tears. Joshua would have loved to know he had an impact on so many people. *Like a drop rippling in the water, I thought.* Perhaps he was there and watching. Pastor Paul, who years earlier helped saved my son and turn his life around, officiated and one-by-one, many of us shared stories of how we remembered and loved Joshua.

We watched the video of Joshua's short but very full life and were reminded of all of the amazing things he had done in his time here. I held Leah's hand as we cried together, witnessing this amazing young man's accomplishments. His smile in the video lit up the room as it had done so many times when he was still with us. At the end of the service I thanked everyone for coming to honor my son. I invited a few of our closest friends to come back to the house for a meal and to

152

continue sharing memories. His best friends Tommy, Andrew, Alex, Brady, and Jacob pored over the scrapbooks I had made of Joshua's life. I watched them laugh as they looked at the photos and memories they had shared with him and I could see they were comforted being together and remembering their beloved friend. They told me Joshua had a way of making each one of them feel special and loved no matter what they were going through. They always knew they had a loyal friend in him and said he was a truly great listener. He was, they said, a safe place to share without fear of being judged.

My purpose had been to teach my son to be to "useful, honorable, compassionate, and to leave this world making some difference that he had lived and lived well" to paraphrase Ralph Waldo Emerson. In the painful aftermath of his death, I understood that he had learned those lessons well. After finding his way back from some painful and poor choices and overcoming one medical crisis after another, Joshua found joy, happiness, and contentment in his life. Knowing he found peace in his last years helped me accept his passing. I also knew I had to find another way to honor his precious life. He once told me his dream of returning to Israel with me and retracing his footsteps together. I made the trip with him, though not in the way he had hoped.

Nine months after Joshua passed away, my girlfriend April accompanied me to Israel, to make a pilgrimage in honor of my son's memory. I thought I was doing this for my son but I came to understand this was exactly what I needed to grieve my loss.

It was very difficult for me to grieve at home. I was the strong one and felt the need to support and encourage those around me. As I always had, I kept myself busy and focused on anything and everything other than the loss of my child. That was a place I was not ready to go yet. I felt emotionally numb and went about my life like a robot, saying all the right things to assure everyone that I was fine. I wasn't fine but was not ready to face the truth. At times I would just sit on my back deck and allow the sadness to seep in but I had a daughter that needed my attention and love.

Taking time to get away was exactly what I needed. After several months being at home I could see that I was stuck and couldn't move forward. I knew I would never move on... but I needed to move forward and begin healing. I hired Yaron, a Messianic Jew, a man born Jewish who converted to Christianity, who was Joshua's and Keith's guide in Israel three years prior. He met us at the Tel Aviv airport with open arms and tears in his eyes.

For the first few days, we toured Haifa and the surrounding area, visiting places Joshua had been. We stopped at a park and were mesmerized by beautiful sculptures entitled "From the Holocaust to Resurrection," depicting the rebirth of hope. We went to the caves in Rosh Hanikra on the Mediterranean Sea, the first of many places where I left some of Joshua's ashes. I wept as I sprinkled some of them at the mouth of the caves as Yaron prayed the Kaddish, a Jewish prayer for the dead. He taught us the response to the Kaddish, "el maleh rachamim," which translates as "God full of compassion."

As I looked out on this beautiful, breezy day, the warm sun on my face, I thought of Joshua, who had described his joy of feeling the ocean spray on his face and listening to the ocean as it "whooshed" in-and-out of the cave. We next visited Akko where, according to the New Testament, the Apostle Paul began many of his missionary trips. Joshua once stood in this same place, seeing himself as a missionary, spreading God's word of love and peace.

At the Carmel Assembly Church, I left ashes in the prayer room. Many of the members remembered Joshua fondly and told me how moved they were by this young man, blind and in a wheelchair, still able to share his loving and joyful spirit with them.

Over the next ten days, I laid my son to rest along the Sea

of Galilee, in Nazareth, at the Wailing Wall in Old Jerusalem, in the Golan Heights, and in the Jordan River where he had once been carried in his wheelchair, down a steep, rocky slope into the waters to be baptized again, in the same place Jesus had been baptized. We followed Joshua's journey into the back-alleys of Bethlehem and walked the hidden paths and doorways to the birthplace of Jesus. As I retraced his path, I imagined Joshua's excitement and awe visiting this holy ground.

Yaron took us to a small shop in Bethlehem where my son purchased a beautiful nativity set for me. I showed the owner a picture of Joshua. He remembered him and, in very broken English, told me he believed my son was a very special young man, chosen by God. He said he was building a new home high on a hill overlooking Bethlehem, invited me to purchase a small olive tree, a symbol of peace, bring it to his home, and place some of Joshua's ashes beneath the tree as I planted it. He said it would be his honor to watch over Joshua in the years to come. I was moved to tears by this incredible act of kindness from a stranger and I understood now why Joshua was drawn to and loved these wonderful and compassionate people.

As we walked through Old Jerusalem along the Via de La Rosa – the way of suffering – I imagined Joshua pushing and pulling his wheelchair along these very narrow, winding, cobblestone streets. I felt his presence everywhere. Though he was blind, Joshua had listened and seen everything with his heart.

At the Holocaust Museum in Yad Vashem in Jerusalem, my grief poured out. I was standing amid this stunning tribute to more than six million lost, innocent souls, reminders of one of the most horrific times in human history. A testament of death, grief, pain, and loss. I was one mother who had lost her only son and the palpable agony of all the mothers who lost their own children overwhelmed me. My heart broke for all of us.

Joshua's favorite moment of his journey to Israel was floating weightless in the Dead Sea. He told me it was the first time in years he felt physically free, not needing to be picked up or carried by someone else. It was a cool, cloudy day in April when Yaron, April, and I arrived there, not a soul in sight. As we put on our bathing suits and headed down to the beach, we saw a lone wheelchair, no one around, just perched on the water's edge as if it waiting for its owner to appear. I froze, a lump in my throat and just stared at the chair. Was this a sign? Where did it come from? Who did it belong to? I was stunned. We went slowly into the sea, fighting the buoyancy as we floated effortlessly because of the dense minerals in the water. I pictured my son's frail body floating next to mine and talked to him. Suddenly I heard Joshua's laughter behind my left ear. In that split second before my brain could bring me into reality, I jumped up, looked around, excited to see my son, but of course he was nowhere to be seen. I came to believe this was God's way of telling me Joshua was no longer suffering, now at peace with his Maker, running around and laughing freely with the other angels. I walked out of the water with a sense of peace I had never experienced. My son was happy, no longer suffering and, for once and for the rest of time, out of his wheelchair.

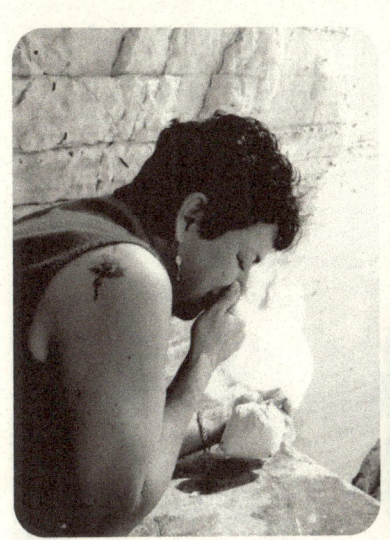

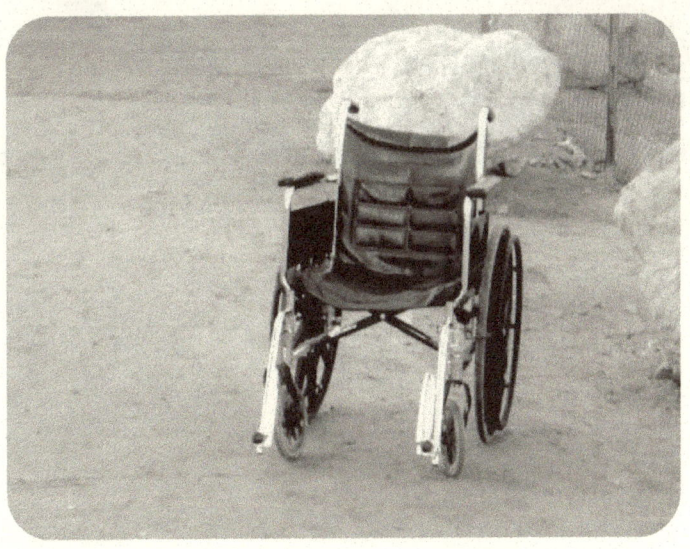

The Last Dance

CHAPTER 13
Losing Leah

"There must be those among us with whom we can
sit down and weep and still be counted as warriors."
—Adrienne Rich

After Joshua was gone it seemed as if he had taken all the oxygen in our lives with him, that critical element allowing all sentient beings to live and breathe. I thought I was prepared. I had known for 17 years, from the time he was diagnosed at the age of six, until his last breath at 23, that he was going to die young. Nothing...nothing could have prepared me for his death nor the prospect of losing my daughter as well. The silence in the house was deafening. I kept walking past his room, looking inside, expecting to see him again, and hear him calling "Mom." I remembered how I used to get annoyed hearing him call me constantly, now wishing I could hear his voice just one more time. With the medical equipment and hospital bed gone I could now remember my boy as a happier and healthier child, free now from the suffering he endured in his final days.

I sometimes laid in his bed, picked up his clothes, trying to inhale some scent of him, believing those gestures might bring him back to me in some spiritual way. In French there is a saying: *"Tu me manques,"* which literally means "You are missing from me." How perfect an expression. Joshua was missing from me, leaving a void – an empty chasm – I truly never wanted to fill. He left a space only he could fill and I would keep that space for him forever.

I went through the motions of daily life. I shopped, cooked, ate, and talked with a few friends, but I did everything in an almost robotic state, with little heart or enthusiasm for anything. I was exhausted, full of despair, and numb. I had raised him and cared for him his entire life, helping him surmount and survive one terrible obstacle after another, at his side through dozens of torturous medical procedures for thousands of days and now it all stopped. My steadfast, silent partner Cliff guided me through the empty weeks following Joshua's death. He listened when I needed to talk and held me tightly when I had nothing to say. Every time I wept, he cried with me and became more of a comfort to Leah when I was unable to give her the support and love she needed. When she spent time in Joshua's room, Cliff saw how much she, too, was missing her big brother and found ways to spend more time with her, make her laugh, and feel valued. I was so grateful to have Bre watching over and caring for Leah, never leaving her side and being the support Leah needed. I wanted to be more present and attentive to Leah, but the darkness surrounding me overshadowed everything else.

Life got even darker. Less than a year after Joshua's death, my eldest sister Denise, who had survived a heart attack a few years earlier, died of colon cancer at the age of 57. She was everything to me, the person who always made me feel very special. Denise had been a rock and tremendous friend to me over the years. Distance dictated that we talk on the phone and I would call her regularly to just catch up. She was a shoulder I could always count on to be in my corner. Before her death, as I had done for our father and for my children, I made a scrapbook commemorating her life and was able to share it with her before she passed. Scrapbooks had become a way for me to offer a celebration of life to those special people in my

160

life who were passing away. I would visit them, no matter where they were on the planet and collect a series of pictures representing all the special moments in their lives. I would return to my home and quickly assemble an ornate and beautiful scrapbook that I would show them before they passed. The joy on their faces always confirmed how validating and uplifting it was for them to see the beautiful life they had lived. On his death bed, my father, with tears in his eyes, told me that he would take the gift of my scrapbook to heaven with him. My sister Denise was the funniest person I knew and a person who could find humor in any situation, even her pending death. She brought up Bon Jovi's song, *"Wanted Dead or Alive'"* something we managed to laugh about as she laid in her bed at the palliative care facility. She left behind a husband, daughter, granddaughter, and the rest of her family who adored her. This was the third very personal death in my life in just three years – my father, my son, and now my sister – each a painful, wrenching loss, but I had to find a way to keep living. I had a daughter who needed me now more than ever.

A month after Joshua passed, Leah was invited to speak to her peers at an annual National Ataxia Foundation conference held in Seattle. As she shared deeply personal and insightful thoughts about living with FA, I watched her, in awe of her courage, strength, and insight. I had never been so proud of my beautiful daughter as I was that day.

Leah, as usual, was dressed beautifully in stylish jeans and a copper colored blouse. She looked out into the audience, the stage lights illuminating her direct gaze and warm smile. *"For those of you who don't know me, my name is Leah Chalcraft and I'm 21. I live here in Seattle and I have Friedreich's Ataxia. I was diagnosed at the age of six. By the age of 10 I needed help walking with a walker and I was having difficulty hearing. By 5th grade I started using a wheelchair fulltime. In the past couple of years, I've noticed that my vision and hearing is diminishing and I have a difficult time using my hands. When I was still a teenager I had mononucleosis and also had a heart attack. I'm telling you this because I want you to know that in spite of all of these challenges, I went to college after high school and graduated with an AA degree in Education which allows me to be a para-educator. I don't need my hands to help kids with reading, spelling, and math."* I watched as the audience sat transfixed. No one looked away and I could see so many faces beaming up at my daughter. *"FA is something we have, it's NOT who we are!"* she said as the audience burst into applause.

Her appearance at the National Ataxia Conference gave her a moment of happiness and a feeling of being respected and appreciated, but Joshua's death brought with it incredibly sad days for us all. Leah was struggling as were we all.

I decided we needed some time together, away from home and away from all the memories within the walls of our home. I suggested we take a trip to Hawaii and when I saw the smile on her face, I knew it was the perfect thing to do. It was April, her birthday month, when she would turn 22 and, as with Joshua, I knew I was on borrowed time with my daughter. When she was diagnosed at the age of six, doctors told me she might only live five to 15 years, but Leah had already far outlived her life expectancy and I wanted to reconnect with her and hopefully create a wonderful memory in whatever time remained.

We arrived in Oahu on a beautiful, sunny day in April and checked into a hotel close to the ocean. We both loved the sun and water and were excited to celebrate in style. We managed to laugh as we struggled to navigate the non-accessible sidewalks and cumbersome paths to the beach and kept smiling when the lifeguard had to help me lift her into a special beach wheelchair and in-and-out of the water. Her regular chair was not able to travel in the sand and the beach was too far away to carry her the whole distance. The water was her happy place, where she could float and feel the warmth of the sun on her skin. As we had for years, we

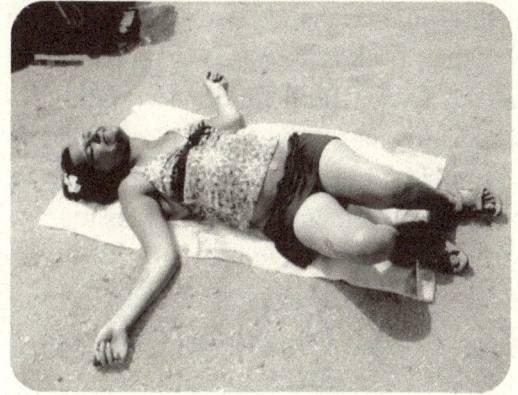

competed to see who could get the darkest tan. Leah had inherited my olive-toned skin and we laughed again as we argued about who was the darkest.

We spoke often of Joshua, both in Hawaii and after we returned home. Eventually we were able to smile and even laugh at the "Joshisms" that popped-up in our conversations, such as how he said "oops" when bumping into a wall or a person. We also cried together when sadness overcame us and I encouraged her to feel the pain and grief of his loss though I myself was

not quite ready to allow myself to feel the depth and breadth of the agony of losing Joshua. Little bits and pieces of grief was all I could handle. Thank God Bre, Leah's caregiver, was in our lives. When I was distracted and mourning the loss of my son, she was a wonderful friend to Leah and kept her busy with shopping,

movies, small parties, visiting friends, and even going to drag clubs. Bre brought fun back into our home and it made me happy when I heard them laughing in Leah's room, gossiping about various friends and family. She was a lifesaver for both of us, giving Leah support and allowing me time to get away and regroup. She became another daughter to me, a daughter from another mother; a kind, generous, and loving person who helped bring us out of the darkness.

Leah honored Joshua in many special ways. She, along with Bre and several of their friends, took part in the Muscular Dystrophy Association Walk and Roll fundraiser and called their group "Team Halo," Joshua's rapper name. With Leah's service dog Bella by her side, they rolled and walked away, laughing about the antics they remembered about Joshua.

The Joshua Tree*

On February 1st, the anniversary of Joshua's passing, Bre and their friend Angie took Leah down to the White river near our home and tossed flowers into the water in memory of Joshua. In December they started what they hoped would be an annual tradition. They found a tree in Federal Way in full view of the freeway and decorated it with Christmas balls

* Two stories have been written on the decorating of this tree in the *Federal Way Mirror*.
2020: https://www.federalwaymirror.com/life/hands-behind-the-holiday-magic-who-decorates-federal-ways-community-tree-for-christmas/
2021: https://www.federalwaymirror.com/news/holiday-tradition-brings-two-families-together/

and streamers in honor of Joshua. All these gestures helped Leah cope with the death of her brother.

While we never specifically talked about her own death, its specter was ever-present. Several years after Leah passed there was an article in our local newspaper about a family who had noticed the tree was no longer decorated and wondered if the person responsible had either moved away or died. They decided to continue the tradition because they loved seeing the special Christmas tree. Bre showed me the article and I contacted the paper and shared how the tradition began. They followed-up with the full story, another way to honor the memory of my children. To this day, every Christmas, the family continues decorating "our" tree.

Keith continued seeing his daughter when it suited him and his new wife Kimberly, enjoying spending time with her. Leah loved having Kimberly cut and color her hair and do all the girly things such as makeup and shopping. Kimberly invited Leah on a trip to San Diego, and I was both amazed and impressed with Kimberly's courage taking Leah on a week-long excursion. Very few people had ever taken my children on even an overnight stay, let alone a longer trip. Though I never got many of the details, the trip turned out to be a much bigger challenge than expected and they came home early. Leah shared how funny it was when her wheelchair got stuck in a manhole as they were trying to cross a street. The chair was too heavy for Kimberly to push it out no matter how hard she tried. Somehow Leah found humor in the fact that no one was stopping to help until finally a good Samaritan rescued them. Even with that challenge and the fact that the trip ended early, Leah remained grateful for the adventure.

In December 2011, we got news that Uncle Alfie was not well. Alfie and Janet had been friends of mine for almost 30 years and I had cared for both of their sons Alex and Andrew, and loved them as much as I loved my own children. I rushed to the hospital where Janet and the boys sat by his side, fully intubated, kept alive by machines. Before he passed away I quietly thanked him for being in our lives. He had been an uncle, almost a second father, to Joshua and Leah and could make anyone laugh about anything. Although Leah wanted to come with me to the hospital, I wanted to spare her another great sorrow so I made the trip alone. On the day of the winter solstice, the shortest and coldest day of the year, Alfie passed away. Janet asked me to eulogize Alfie at his memorial service and I was honored to comply.

Through the loss of her grandpa, brother, Tauntie Denise, and her Uncle Alfie, Leah's service dog Bella comforted her. She seemed to sense Leah's sadness and would jump on her bed and lie by her side for hours at a time. I often heard Leah talking with her and sharing her thoughts and feelings.

One warm, June evening we noticed Bella was not feeling well and having difficulty standing up. It came on so suddenly. Cliff picked her up, laid her on the back seat of our van, and the three of us took Bella to the vet. I could see the panic on Leah's face and tried to minimize her concern by assuring her we would do everything possible to make Bella well. But as we all feared, the news was not good. Bella had cancer and was not going to recover. I looked at my distraught daughter and told her the most compassionate thing we could do was to put her to sleep and take away her suffering, but it was her decision to make. This was her dog, her longtime companion for six years, her best friend who once saved her life. Leah told the vet to give her the medicine that would end Bella's suffering. Cliff had to leave the room, unable to witness this overwhelmingly sad moment. Leah put her arms around Bella's neck, hugged her, and told her how much she loved her. We sat with this beautiful dog until she took her last breath. I had no words to comfort my daughter who had suffered so many losses in recent years. I could only sit with her and hold her tight as we cried together. The loss of a pet, especially a service dog, is as painful as losing a member of the family. They are family and, in some ways, far more perfect than humans. They love unconditionally, have no judgment, never hold a grudge, and ask nothing of their family except perhaps the occasional scratch or treat. That was our Bella, a most beautiful creature inside and out.

Shortly after losing Bella, when Leah was 24, she began complaining profusely about pain in her back and tailbone. She had been fairly active, living a full social life, but began spending more and more time in bed to help relieve the pressure in her back. There were many days when she did not get out of bed at all. She became depressed and found little joy in her life. She talked about getting married, having babies, and having a job as her friends were doing.

My heart kept breaking, knowing she would never experience any of these things. She was so weak and helpless, and I felt helpless as well, aching inside that there was little I could do to relieve my daughter's misery. I often sat with her, watching television or a movie. A friend suggested I watch a film called *"The Way,"* a father's journey on the Camino de Santiago in the northern regions of Spain. Knowing Leah loved to travel, we watched the movie together and she later told me she wanted to take that journey with me. I loved her sense of adventure and the fact that even at this point in her life she still had hopes and dreams.

I promised I would honor her wish and take her with me on the Camino someday. I think in that moment she understood what I meant. She had witnessed her brother's passing and how I had honored him by taking his ashes to Israel. I sensed she knew she would go with me as I had taken the journey with Joshua.

I sought help from her doctor for the pain she was experiencing, but he only wanted to medicate her. We then went to an acupuncturist but found little relief there. Her pain continued and my anxiety grew with each passing day. The search for finding her relief went on for almost a year and I rarely left her side. I read her the entire *Twilight* series, but the distractions Bre and I attempted were not enough to comfort her. We ordered a new gel cushion for her wheelchair that offered a little relief, but not enough. We massaged her back and tailbone daily and gave her Advil to help with the swelling, but everything we tried was only temporary and brought her little lasting relief. In mid-December, 2012, about a year after her back pain began, Leah started having terrible muscle spasms. She screamed in pain as Bre and I put her in her wheelchair and drove to the hospital. I called Keith to meet us there. She was weak and crying out with each spasm. The doctors gave her muscle relaxants, but after examining her said there was little they could do. They could not determine what was causing the spasms but thought perhaps the rod in her back had somehow dislodged. They said she would not survive anesthesia or surgery because her lungs and heart were now extremely weak. She would have to learn to live with the pain. They recommended we take her home, begin hospice care and keep her comfortable.

There is no word to describe what I was feeling watching my daughter suffer. Is there a word to adequately convey what a parent feels seeing their child suffer? She had already experienced so much loss...her ability to walk, the use of her hands, the loss of her beloved brother, her grandfather, her aunt, her uncle, and her Bella...so much pain. If I could have absorbed all her suffering, I would have done it in a heartbeat. But I was helpless to do anything. I only watched as she slowly fell asleep from the drugs. Cliff and I gently lifted her from the hospital bed and into her wheelchair and took her home. As we placed Leah back in her bed, I called hospice to set up an appointment for the next day.

I did not allow my mind to even consider the inevitable future. This was not the time to fall apart. I was determined to be strong and hold it together for the sake of my daughter. I pushed all the darkest thoughts and emotions into a corner of my mind, to a very deep place where I could not reach them. There would be time later to feel this excruciating pain. My heart was still broken from losing Joshua three and a half years earlier and I was terrified if I allowed myself to feel more anguish, I would crumble into little pieces on the floor.

Some friends said the predictable and obligatory things people say in moments like these: "I don't know how you do it," "I can't imagine what you are going through," and there was always someone offering up the improbable statement, "God doesn't give you more than you can handle." Those particular words I found uniquely troubling. They made me feel small and weak because I did not think for a moment that I could "handle" any of this and I surely did not want to. I know people meant well, but their words fell on my completely shattered heart. My only living child was dying. Sometimes just sitting with someone in the darkness and saying nothing is the most comforting thing a friend can do.

When facing a situation that felt insurmountable, I tried to remember I only had to take one step at a time and, by doing that, we would all get through it. This is how I managed to survive this far, more than a decade of helping my children overcome such enormous obstacles and challenges. If I had done it up until now, I could do it going forward, taking one step at a time. The best predictor of future behavior is looking at our past. I had done well, both for myself and for my children."

As I had done when Joshua's death was imminent, I began planning for the inevitable, preparing for organ donations, cremation, and a memorial service to honor her memory. Taking care of details and getting organized kept me busy and gave me some small sense of control when I had none over my daughter's fate. This was my way of coping and keeping my misery at bay. I knew how to organize things. I did not know how to reckon with the loss of my Leah.

Two arduous and anguishing weeks passed and I invited some of Leah's friends to visit to help distract and keep her mind busy. She seemed to enjoy those times but had little energy to talk and the pain medications were taking a toll on her fragile body. She spent almost every day in bed and slept most of the time. Bre did everything possible to keep Leah comfortable and Leah loved the time they had together. It was almost Christmas and we decorated our house and our tree, something Leah always loved. Bre decorated Leah's room with little green lights and helped her entertain her friends.

On Friday, December 21, 2012, the day of the winter solstice and the darkest day of the year, Leah awoke, listless and unable to be picked up and placed in her shower chair. Bre came out to tell me she could not move Leah and would give her a sponge bath instead. I walked into her bedroom and saw my poor, little girl suffering, unable to lift a finger and still whimpering in pain. I knew what had to be done. I held her close in my arms and told her everything would be okay. I promised her she would not be suffering much longer and told her how I loved her. I assured her she was not alone and that Bre would hold her until I came back into the room. I saw tears in Bre's eyes as she told me without uttering a word that she understood what I was saying to our beloved Leah. We could not allow the pain and suffering to continue.

I called the hospice nurse and told her Leah was not doing well and asked her to come see her as soon as possible. Within a few hours she was in our home, telling us Leah was not likely to recover and to begin giving her liquid morphine every half hour. I heard her words and saw what was happening, signs I did not want to acknowledge. Three-and-a-half years had passed since I took part in this ritual with Joshua and I now had to relive my daughter going through the same passage. Giving her the morphine was the kindest thing I could do, but I felt I had failed my daughter by being unable to make her better, by not finding a remedy for her pain and suffering. I had always been a diligent advocate for my children throughout their lives. How could I not find a solution for her now? The drugs I had to give her would finally relieve her pain, but would also take her away from me forever and leave me in more pain than I thought I could absorb. This was not the time to think about that. I stayed focused on trying to give my daughter any happiness and relief I could find.

Family and friends were again invited to come sit with Leah. I placed chairs in her room so she could hear our conversations about the good memories people wanted to share. She was in a drug-induced coma, but I believed she could still hear what we were saying. I sat next to her beautiful head in a place I would not share with anyone. I kept touching her still warm body, whispering in her ear how much I loved her and telling her she would soon once again be with her beloved brother dancing in the streets of heaven, no longer in pain and no longer suffering. I told her I would be okay and she did not have to hold on for me. I would see them again when my time came, but for now everyone she ever loved – including her Bella – would be waiting to greet her.

At 10 p.m. on December 21, I felt my child take her final breath and saw the color drain from her face. Once again, Keith and I held onto each other, sobbing over the loss of our second child. We were broken. My world, which had somehow kept turning after Joshua's death, stopped. I finally allowed my pain and rage to swallow me whole. I did not want comfort. I wanted to be alone and feel all the emotions I had managed to suppress for years, but it was almost too much weight to bear.

Although I knew this moment would come, I still felt unprepared. I took a deep breath and sat with her for a long time, in the darkness. It is such an honor to be with someone passing from this world to the next. I believe she felt safe in my arms and was at peace when she let go. When I was ready, I kissed Leah and thanked her for the beautiful life she shared with me. I wanted to get busy, as was my way, to avoid the depth of sadness swallowing me. Instead I made one phone call to the hospice care nurse and allowed others to handle anything else needing to be done. Time in those final moments was a precious gift I gave myself.

Later, I called family and friends as Bre reached out to Leah's friends to invite them to the memorial service in a couple of weeks. My sister Julie, niece Liane, and my best friend Marie and my first husband Gary and his daughter Selina who was Joshua's great love and a sister for Leah, all flew in from Canada. As I entered the church, I was again comforted by some 600 people, all touched in different ways by Leah in her brief 25 years. It was a beautiful service and several people spoke about Leah with deep love and affection. I sat and listened, but remained in my own insulated bubble, protected by numbness and a necessary detachment, unable to believe my daughter was gone. My body was there, but my mind was in its own self-induced coma.

Many friends brought meals and I was grateful not to have to cook. I have little memory of what we did together. We went downtown to Seattle's Pike Place Market on a sunny, crisp January afternoon. As always, the market was crowded with people and an abundance of beautiful flowers and food everywhere, seasonal bounty from dozens of local farmers. It was only a temporary distraction. The house was brimming with people, but still felt empty. We shared funny memories of Leah which I enjoyed, but after the stories were told, I had to remember she was gone.

I am certain everyone came to comfort me, but in those first months, I was unable to be comforted. My family stayed for almost a week and I welcomed the silence when they left. Their presence was comforting and a beautiful distraction but also stirred up old habits of my need to comfort them, and I had neither the energy nor desire to give anything of myself to anyone. With the memorial service over and my friends and family having returned to their lives, I just wanted to be alone.

Cliff went back to his job in the operations department of Delta Airlines and I stayed home...alone, lost, aimless, and empty. I walked around our house, which no longer felt like a home without either of my children living there. I felt I no longer had any purpose in life, as if I was a blank slate with nothing to be written on it.

I had no idea what to do with all the free time and space suddenly surrounding me. I never had time to myself - ever. I found it almost impossible to concentrate on even reading a book, something I once enjoyed doing. But if I started reading, I would inevitably start reading out loud as I had done with both of my children, so I rarely got past a few pages of anything. Friends came by to see me and though I knew they meant well and tried to comfort me, I had no energy or desire to talk to anyone. I traveled to Canada to visit my family, something I had always loved, but that gave me no joy. I sat in the depth of my sorrow and thought about my children. Sometime in those months of emptiness, I read a quote by James Baldwin: "Not everything that is faced can be changed, but nothing can be changed until it is faced." Almost four months had passed since Leah's death and that quote kept reverberating in my head. I had to face the dreaded truth. My children were gone and I had to find a way to move forward, face the pain of my loss, and imagine I could be happy again.

For the last 25 years my entire identity was tied to Joshua and Leah, taking care of them, trying to inspire them, pushing them to take risks, and encouraging them to live the happiest lives they could despite the terrible challenges they faced. Who was I without my precious children? I was no one. I had no identity if I could not be Joshua and Leah's mother. I knew how to navigate my world when they were in it, but the void left behind when they died left me rudderless. I wondered how the world could continue revolving since mine had crumbled and shattered into a million fragmented pieces, a puzzle waiting to be put back together.

The emptiness I felt in their absence was a world without oxygen where I sometimes had to remind myself to breathe. Then my grief turned into regret and guilt. Despite my family and friends showering me with praise about how I raised my children, doubt found its way to me. Had I been the best mom? Did I do enough for and with Leah? Had I done everything... everything possible to help her at the end of her days? She never seemed to get enough time and attention from me. I blamed myself for not trying to better understand my daughter. We were such different people, my quiet, solitary daughter with her extroverted, always busy mother. I should have taken more time, more time to listen, and just be present with her. Though I was consumed with self-recrimination, I dared not allow the deeply buried feelings of sadness to surface. When the agony of losing my children arose, I shut it down, certain if I did release the unbearable pain it might kill me. Perhaps that is what I wanted, to be with them...gone.

The silence in the house was deafening, the quietude unbearable. It was the loudest noise I had ever heard, stillness echoing from my children's bedrooms. I welcomed the sound of our two small dogs, barking with excitement and wagging their tails when I returned home from some menial errand. I left the television on all day, even when I left the house so I could hear it when I came back to a house devoid of my children. I watched the dogs sitting by the door, waiting for either Joshua or Leah to come in behind me as they had done thousands of times before. They too missed the children. Cliff continued to be my rock, a strong shoulder to lean on, a man who asked nothing of me. He listened when I needed to talk or just sat with me in the dark when I had nothing to say. I wanted to stay in the gloom I now inhabited, a dark house where my children once lived, assured if I remained in that place, I would be able to keep them close. I was afraid if I ever left, I might forget how they looked, smelled, talked, and laughed, something I could never allow to happen. I was numb, in shock, and lost.

Everlasting Embrace

PART FOUR

CHAPTER 14

The Gifts of the Camino...
A Pilgrimage Toward Healing

Live life in such a way that each day is a pilgrimage and each step a journey to a sacred place.
—Sherrie Frank

I am still amazed at our capacity to endure incredible loss and grief and our ability to live through it even though it doesn't seem possible. In my heart I believed there would be a life ahead where this pain would not be so crippling. But there is no way to know or feel it when you are inside it. As I began navigating through the pain of loss and grief I also discovered amazing gifts that I could never have dreamed possible. Had I allowed myself the luxury of staying stuck in my grief, I doubt that I would have uncovered the many gifts that came from the great sorrow.

Losing Joshua was agonizing, but with Leah alive and needing me more every day, my life still had purpose. For 25 years, my entire life had been centered around my children who needed care and attention almost every hour of every day. My daily routine of ensuring they had food, were able to get to the bathroom, get dressed, go to school, make doctor's appointments, find activities where they could participate, and keep up their spirits was my reason for living. Now both were gone. Sometimes I would go into their rooms, sit on their beds, and just stare into the nothingness of my life, or hold a piece of their clothing and inhale their scents. I thought if I stayed there, I could keep them close to me. Having lived one way for decades and suddenly that life ends left me utterly lost, confused, without purpose, and wondering if there is any way to go on living or even any reason to keep breathing. If my life had been upended by the loss of my parents or even my husband, I might have seen that as the natural order of things. We are not supposed to outlive our children, but in truth there is no natural order of things. I had tried with every fiber of my being to "watch them live and not watch them die." But they were both gone now and there was nothing to watch any longer. I was untethered and truly, immeasurably desolate.

As with Joshua, I remember almost nothing of the details of my life after Leah's death, only the awareness that everything had changed and I felt empty...alive, but dead inside. I recall putting myself on autopilot. Bills still had to be paid, appointments kept, food bought and prepared, and dogs attended to, but even our dog Sophie seemed lost, wandering in-and-out of the children's rooms and constantly searching for Leah. She still seemed excited whenever I returned home, but kept going to the door expecting Leah to follow me. Cliff, ever my steady, strong, and silent partner, catered to anything I needed, but the thing I needed most was my children back.

I began to crawl very slowly out of the abyss. I remembered a promise I once made to Leah, to bring her remains with me on the Camino de Santiago in northern Spain, an arduous, physical journey I would need to take if I was ever to move forward emotionally. I recalled Leah and I watching the movie, "The Way," where the father decides to walk the ancient, 500-mile spiritual trail to retrace his son's steps and eventually scatter his son's ashes in the sea at the end. After the movie, Leah shared that she would love to take that journey with me. We had always enjoyed travelling together and this seemed like an amazing adventure to her. I promised her I would take her with me, both knowing it would be in spirit alone that she would accompany me.

After her death, I wanted to honor my daughter's memory as I had done for my son when I took his remains to Israel. My friend Alisa suggested we go to a seminar given by a priest in Seattle, a man who had walked the Camino many times. Listening to him talk about his experience awakened my curiosity, a feeling I had not had for a very long time. In the four months since Leah's passing, I had been numb, unable to feel anything other than sadness. He spoke of his life-changing, spiritual journey and I felt a warmth inside as if my body was beginning to thaw and come alive again. In that moment, I reawakened to the power of the pilgrimage I did when Joshua passed away. It reminded me of the magical and healing power of my journey to honor our life together. I desperately hoped it would be realized once again.

I decided I would walk the Camino in September 2013 and carry Leah's ashes, leaving them along the way.

The Camino de Santiago, known in English as the "Way of St. James," is a network of pilgrimages leading to the shrine of the apostle St. James the Great in the Cathedral of Santiago de Compostela in northwestern Spain. According to tradition, the remains of the saints are buried there and thousands of people follow the route as a means of spiritual growth and renewal, something I desperately needed. I took baby steps preparing for my journey, first selecting a date, then applying to the local pilgrim's society for the necessary Compostela passports. I applied for two, one for me and one for Leah. The passports are stamped at every place you stay and every church you go into along the way to prove you have, indeed, walked "The Way" to qualify as a pilgrim.

I met with a local woman who had walked the Camino several times to help me plan for the trip. Everything I would need had to be carried in a backpack, ideally no heavier than 12 pounds. She suggested I bring comfortable hiking shoes, basic toiletries, a couple pairs of socks, shorts, tops, a sleeping bag liner, two water bottles, and comfortable sandals to rest my weary feet in the evening. More importantly, she reminded me to come equipped with ibuprofen and plenty of Compeed bandages for my inevitably blistered feet. I had never heard of these before, but they are specially designed for hiking, guaranteed to deliver instant relief and healing. They would come in very handy on my trek. She also recommended bringing two walking sticks and healthy snacks.

By the time I finished packing, I was six pounds over her suggested limit and told myself that was not enough to make a difference. I was wrong. Each day along my journey, I would look at my backpack and consider what I could live without. I left behind a belt, some hair gel, a heavy pack of wipes, and a black bathing suit. I thought about how those seemingly small items, when added together, weighed me down and though they brought me some comfort, were impeding my journey. That gesture, getting rid of unnecessary things, made me consider my life and begin thinking about the emotional burdens I had been carrying and needed to expunge. I did no special physical training, no walking long distances, or any kind of power-lifting. Though I was mentally exhausted and emotionally drained after the deaths of both of my children, I was in remarkably good physical shape. After all, I had been lifting my children in and out of their wheelchairs and in and out of their baths for more than 20 years. I felt prepared.

On September 24, 2013, nine months after Leah's passing, I got on a plane and flew to Madrid, Spain and took a train north to the beginning point of my trek from Sarria. I had decided to walk only 100 miles of the 500-mile Camino, which was the minimum required to receive the "Compostela" (aka Pilgrim's Credential/certificate). It was the most popular distance for beginner pilgrims to walk. I had never done anything like this and was completely unsure if I could even walk 100 miles, but somehow believed I would be fine. My children had taught me something about courage and strength. Upon arrival I followed other pilgrims who seemed to know where they were going and found an "albergue" marked "peregrinos albergue" that translates to "hostels for pilgrims." I had been told by fellow travelers this sign indicated cheap and clean rooms, designed for weary and often wet travelers. I barely slept, adrenaline pumping through my veins with my excitement to begin walking.

It was September 25th, what would have been Joshua's 28th birthday, when I set out on the first day of my walk. I didn't plan it this way, to begin my journey on my son's birthday. I stopped in my tracks before I even began walking as I realized the date's significance – the first gifts of many I would experience. Was it a coincidence or Joshua's way of communicating with me? I still desperately missed him and thought about what a 28-year-old would be doing at this point in his life. My heart felt heavy and sad. He was the one who should be traveling the world, finding himself and having adventures, and instead I was making the trek. It seemed neither right nor fair. This would be the only day I contemplated Joshua's life. Going forward, my pilgrimage would honor Leah. That was my purpose for being there.

With daylight breaking and the sky becoming light, the forest was a magical, mystical fairy land. As I walked along the path, I found the first memorial altar where I would leave some of Leah's ashes, along with a small, glass dragonfly. A symbol of courage and dignity, Leah's beloved dragonflies held great meaning for her. The first step, as it is often said, is the most difficult as I prepared to leave some of Leah's ashes at the sacred altar. I stood and pondered the wonderful but terribly challenging life Leah lived. As I reflected on my daughter's life, other feelings began to surface. I allowed myself to feel the anger I suppressed when my children were alive. I was angry about the life she would never live, the babies she would not have, the husband she craved, but would never marry. She had been cheated from so many of the passages of life young people experience and dream about. It was all so unfair. I realized as I prepared to leave some of her ashes at this site that I had never allowed myself to feel sorry for her while she was alive. My focus was always on trying to protect her and keep her spirits up. Now, holding her ashes in my hands, I gave myself permission to acknowledge my emotions. I wept as I began to face my true feelings and believed as I cried that this was, hopefully, the beginning of my healing.

As I continued my 100-mile journey, my heart and soul opened to other thoughts and feelings I never allowed myself to experience over 25 years. It was hard to acknowledge these things as I walked and, even now, it is difficult to write about them without feeling great shame. I thought about the relief I felt after Leah passed and was overcome with guilt as they emerged. What did that say about me? What mother would feel relief after the death of their child? What would people think if they knew what I felt? I tried to banish those thoughts from my mind. I was not ready to accept or acknowledge I was exhausted after more than two decades of caring for my very special needs children or deserved to feel a sense of relief and release from those burdens.

I recalled a conversation I had with my best friend Marie, six months before Leah died. I was completely exhausted and wondered out loud how long I could continue to care for my daughter. At that time, I quickly shoved those feelings back into an iron-clad corner of my mind. It was not the time to say or even think such things. I was deep into the battle for her life and she needed me more than ever. I had compassion-fatigue and had given so much for an entire generation. I was burned out. But here on the Camino, I was free, perhaps for the first time in my life and this was, finally, the right time and place to surrender to the truth of how difficult life had been. I now had no one to take care of and began to give myself permission to bow to both the mental and physical hardships of my life. How dare a mother claim they were relieved in the wake of their children's deaths? But...I was.

I thought about all the things I sacrificed to care for Joshua and Leah. It still felt wrong to think those things. Almost any mother would have done what I did, but my suppressed feelings needed release. I was never able to travel freely or fully devote myself to my career. I had to plan and even over-plan anytime I went away. I always had to be ready to cancel or change direction in case a medical emergency required my attention or Keith changed his mind about caring for them. There were hundreds of those times, a veritable endless list of crises every year they were alive. During that period, I did what had to be done without complaint, never wanting Joshua or Leah to feel they were a burden. I not only took care of their physical needs but tried with every fiber of my being to care for their emotional needs, buoying their spirits and giving every ounce of my energy into being positive and happy, even if I did not feel it. Now the solitude of the Camino enabled the long-buried truth to come out. I was worn down and many times in my life with my children, the responsibility was too much to bear. I resented not only what my children were going through, but what I was also having to face. I sometimes turned to food or evenings out with friends to lessen my pain. While those things brought temporary relief, now being alone on this sacred road, being honest with myself, I felt the promise of real forgiveness.

Continuing on I saw small altars, pillars, and loving tributes reflecting the memories, grief, and burdens of thousands of pilgrims who walked this road for centuries before me. This was a beautiful reminder that I was not alone in my grief and never will be as long as I walk this earth. Every time I stopped to leave more of her ashes and a miniature dragonfly behind, I shed more tears that, for the first time since losing her, flowed freely. Finally I allowed myself to feel

185

the incalculably deep sense of sorrow, and I mourned for the life my baby girl was never able to live, for the intense pain she suffered in the final year of her life. I began to forgive myself for being unable to relieve her pain.

Still, on that first day of the Camino, it was now clear how uncomfortable it had been for me to feel sadness and how, for most of my life, I built exterior walls of smiles and happiness to avoid exposing myself or allowing myself to be depressed. I could not allow my children to see my pain amid their own suffering. I never wanted them to feel guilt, sadness, or any responsibility for the life we were living because of their disease. I had to hold my feelings in check as long as they lived. I convinced myself I had no right to feel sad, seeing the suffering of so many around me in this world, especially my children. I called my sister Julie at the end of my first day and she cried with me, knowing how important this pilgrimage was for me. She did not try to fix or console me, which gave me great comfort, but allowed me to cry, shedding tears I suppressed for so long. She was my safe haven and understood I needed her to sit in the darkness with my pain. Though we were separated by thousands of miles, she was still by my side, holding me up.

As I considered my relationship with Leah and the burdens I carried, I learned I needed to talk less and listen more. The noise had kept me from feeling what I was uncomfortable feeling when I was with her. I often felt restless because she was so quiet and I talked to fill the emptiness. I wished, reflecting on our lives, I would have been able to sit with her in her silent moments and just "be" with her. She wanted "quiet" time with me. It was fulfilling for her, but I struggled sitting with quietness. It freed too much time and space and allowed emotions to creep in, emotions with which I never wanted to reckon until now. I needed to learn to slow down and try and be comfortable in the stillness...and let in the pain. Yet another healing gift of the Camino.

Fifty miles into my walk along the Camino, about halfway through my journey, I stopped to rest in a field filled with bright sunflowers. A lone dragonfly flew by and hovered next to me as I walked another couple of miles. I believed this was my Leah letting me know she was now happy and free, and it gave me great comfort. I always felt her walking beside me, revealing many truths to me. She was telling me life does not have to be perfect to still be wonderful. She reminded me that despite her terrible challenges, we had wonderful times together...dancing with her friends, putting on plays, singing in the school talent show, modeling, camping, and enjoying our road trips to Canada. She was sharing the gifts I had given her throughout her life and the gratitude she felt for the beautiful meaningful times we shared.

In the evenings, after walking 10 to 15 miles, I showered and prepared for a delicious meal. It did not matter who you had met or where they had come from, we all sat at communal tables and shared stories about our journeys. There was a quiet vulnerability in the room and I was inspired by every person, each one in transition or grieving for different reasons. They spoke of a lost job they loved, an unwanted divorce, abuse, retirement, or the loss of loved ones. They had come to honor those whom they had lost and try to work through their sorrow. I was in that last group, trying with every step to heal my deep sadness. Tears and comfort were given and received by complete strangers. It was a safe place to share. I no longer felt the need to put up walls or protect myself or others with feigned happiness. I did not have to be strong or smile or be positive or upbeat for anyone traveling with me. I was finally able to feel the grief I had been pushing away while my children were alive and mourn them now that they are both gone.

Every day I walked, Selina Kozub, Joshua's special love and a true sister to Leah, emailed a beautiful picture of flowers she had picked and wrote a special message of love and encouragement.

Excerpts from one of her offerings:

Hi Mamma,

"*For day eight of your journey, on October 1ˢᵗ, your flowers are the small flowers that make up the beautiful center of a sunflower. Your little boy and little girl aren't here anymore, but you are and you're not just surviving, you're thriving. For you to be conquering Spain is a miracle. If at all on this journey you were asking God for a miracle to get you through this, this is it. You are the miracle.*"

Selina's words were loving and empowering, helping carry me along the journey.

At the end of my walk, fellow pilgrims and I found our way into the old city of Santiago de Compostelo where a pilgrim's mass is held daily at noon. Our names were called out and a certificate issued, simply indicating "it is accomplished," and indeed it was. As I entered the city and looked up at the immense Cathedral de Santiago, I cried again, thinking of what I had achieved as I physically felt some of my burdens lifting. I had honored my precious daughter and left most of her sacred ashes along this holy trail. I had brought her with me in the only way I could and found some measure of peace and the beginning of healing for my broken heart. I felt so proud I had successfully walked this pilgrimage in her honor.

So many times, when the walk was difficult and the pain in my poor blistered feet distracted me, I remembered something Cliff emailed to me on my second day of walking after I sent him a picture of my aching feet. He wrote "my poor babe with her blisters of love and courage." In those moments, I was reminded of the pain and suffering of my Leah and of her strength and courage and perseverance, rarely complaining. I needed to be strong as she had always been.

The hostel in Santiago was old and worn down, but still comfortable and welcoming. Many of us weary warriors sat outside on the deck after dinner and listened as several pilgrims played guitar and began to sing. We organically began telling our stories as we had over the past few weeks. There was a young girl who had suffered terrible abuse from her stepfather and walked the Camino to process her rage and feelings of abandonment towards him and her mother. A young man from Australia, with long, dirty dreadlocks and ragged clothing, had walked barefoot along the entire 500 miles, up steep mountain paths and through dense forests and fields carrying his mother's ashes. He had lost a shoe on his first day and believed it was a sign he should walk barefoot along the entire Camino. He and his mother had planned to walk together, but she died of cancer before they could make the journey. He broke down sobbing and I instinctively went to him, held him tightly, and cried with him.

When I shared the story of my children and the purpose of my pilgrimage, I began to cry again. This time my barefoot traveler came over and held me. I somehow felt safer in the arms of strangers than I had felt back home. When Leah's friends and my family and friends came to offer comfort, I often ended up comforting them. I had spent more than 20 years giving love, sustenance, and comfort to my children and others. That was my default way of coping. I was good at that and not so successful at letting others take care of me. Here on the Camino I was able to grieve openly without feeling compelled to protect others. This was another of many unexpected gifts that I would cherish. I was in a safe place and able, for the first time in decades, to be vulnerable.

At the end of my 100-mile journey along the Camino, some of the walls I spent decades building were beginning to come down. The sadness, anger, and even resentment were now being validated and acknowledged. I was finally beginning to realize it was okay not to be okay. In the past, when Joshua and Leah were alive, every time people told me they were sorry for my loss, I would answer with "It's okay, you don't have to be sad," I was now learning to accept kindness by simply saying "thank you."

After resting for a couple of days, I kept following the path and continued to Finisterre, "The End of the Earth," a coastal fishing town where people once believed the world ended. Traditionally, pilgrims come to this sacred place to rid themselves of burdens, symbolized by burning shoes, clothing, or leaving a stone to represent what they wished to leave behind. As probably millions of pilgrims had done for centuries I, too, carried a stone with me along the 100-mile journey. The stone sits in our pockets to remind us why we are walking, and it is a symbol of the burdens we carry. I had chosen a stone engraved with a dragonfly, which I knew Leah would have loved. I was also holding on to some of her ashes, not quite ready to let her go until I reached Finisterre and the ocean. Along the way I found a beautiful statue of St. James, patron saint of the Camino, and felt compelled to stop. I put in my earphones and looked out onto the vast blue sea and listened to our song "Hero" by Mariah Carey. I remembered how every time it would come on the radio Leah and I would crank it up and sing together. It was our song. As I listened carefully to the words, probably for the first time, tears poured down my face as she spoke very clearly to me. I had always thought of her as my hero and that is why the song was so meaningful. As I sat in the sunlight, eyes closed, thinking of her, she clearly spoke to me and said "Mom, for me, you have always been my hero." My burden was lifted, that of not being "enough" for her and I realized my little girl saw me in a different light than I had seen myself when she was alive. This was the gift Leah gave me.

It was a cloudy, breezy day when I found the cross next to the lighthouse on the coast, and I wondered if I should leave all her ashes there or bring some back to Santiago with me. This was the end of this part of our journey. Life would never be the same. The clouds suddenly parted as warm sunshine poured out onto the rocky cliff, another gift from my daughter, telling me I must leave everything here. I placed the rest of Leah's ashes, a picture of Bre and Leah, a letter from Alisa, and the stone with the dragonfly at the foot of the cross. I spent several hours alone, thanking Leah for the gift of her life. I wept and felt Leah's arms wrap around me, assuring me she was well, free to move, free of pain, and blessing me to move forward and keep walking. I had honored her wish by bringing her with me on the Camino and she had somehow given me the gift of "time," permission to move on with my life in the best way I could until I could see her again.

I accomplished what I came to do, honor my daughter and allow feelings of loss and joy to coexist along my journey. I felt the overwhelming sadness in my life begin to lift...the weight of decades seeing my children suffering and the burden of the sacrifices I had made to give them their best lives. I knew joy was finding its way back into my life. The Camino gave me the opportunity to smile and even have hope again.

On October 4, 2013, I boarded a plane in Madrid and headed home to Seattle. Though my physical body was leaving, the sacred experience of the Camino was now deeply embedded in my soul. That pilgrimage, even with the blisters, gave me hope for the first time in almost a year. I knew someday I would return. I finally knew I was strong enough to survive.

CHAPTER 15

The Journey Continues

"Grief never ends, but it changes. It's a passage, not a place to stay."
—anonymous

I returned home after 14 days away and, while nothing had physically changed, I was different. Apprehensive about being in the house without Joshua and Leah, I feared missing their constant need for me. I was, at first, afraid of the silence. My daily rituals over the previous 25 years filled every hour. Their needs—whether helping in the bathroom, dressing for school, driving them somewhere, or feeding them—defined my life. But they no longer needed me.

An important thing I needed to do was step away from all things related to Ataxia such as local support and Facebook groups. In the wake of their deaths, I did not want to remember my children's illness or their suffering. I donated their wheelchairs and our specially equipped van to a family that needed them. They had served their purpose in our lives and were now needed to help others.

When grief overwhelmed me, I allowed myself to just sit, cry, and feel the sadness, to succumb for a little while to the darkness. I knew intuitively if I fought the urge to feel my grief it would consume me, so I wisely chose to let it in and pray that in time it would diminish.

The emptiness and quiet in the house were still unsettling. I kept waiting for voices that never called for me to bring them something, the sounds of their friends in their rooms, music that never played, the sight of either of my children in their wheelchairs...now all gone from our home.

I tried to keep busy and distract myself by focusing on my Pampered Chef business. My heart was no longer in the business, but I continued putting on parties and my consultants and customers helped and encouraged me. I felt joy in this and it was a healthy distraction, easy and something I was good at. It was not the right time to make any major changes in my life. I had survived the most momentous change any parent can suffer, so returning to something familiar and safe felt like the right thing to do. I told myself to "fake it till I felt it," but everywhere I went and everything I did reminded me of the times I shared with my children.

The one thing I was unable to prepare for, something I never thought about or anticipated, was how to fill the empty spaces inside me once my children were gone. I never planned for that inevitable future. I was used to living in a state of unending crisis. I felt my true purpose in life disappeared along with my children. I was no longer needed. Who was I without them?

The first year without either of my children was, inevitably, one of the hardest, going through the firsts of every celebration; Christmas, Easter, Thanksgiving, and birthdays without them. For the first Christmas in decades, I did not put up a single decoration. I saw no possible joy in it and little reason to celebrate. It would mean nothing without them, without being able to see the smiles on their faces.

On their birthdays and the anniversaries of their passing, I sometimes posted pictures on Facebook, wanting to remind others they had lived. I knew I would never forget them, but I wanted to ensure others would not either. It was evident in the hundreds of comments from family and friends they were not forgotten, which gave me great comfort

Close friends and family were often afraid to even mention my children, worried it would make me sad. Some said they felt guilty knowing their children were still alive and worried that talking about their own children might trigger the painful reality of my loss. In those moments, I assured them it was okay to talk about Leah and Joshua, that it made me feel good knowing they had not been forgotten. It was a gift listening as my friends shared memories and funny stories about my children. Joshua loved to wear white as a sign of righteousness and humility and desired to be just like Jesus. He would literally stop strangers and ask if they knew Jesus and did they know that Jesus loves them. My dear friend "Auntie" Wanda recounted the story of how Joshua asked her one day to shave off his full beard. She knew he was so proud of it and asked him why he wanted her to do that. His reply was, "Because I don't want anyone to mistake me for Jesus." Holding back her giggles for another time, Wanda promptly shaved every hair off his chin. His innocence and sincere reply has kept us giggling many times over the years. That was my son.

I had built strong relationships over the previous 25 years and felt I had all the support I needed from family and friends. I accepted their help even when I did not feel like it. This was a way to stay connected and I needed that. They had expressed their need to feel like they could be a support as well. I became somewhat obsessed thinking about the lives they could not live, about the injustice of all of the things they never got to experience: marriage, children, and careers. Sometimes my sadness and anger seemed more than I could bear. On my worst days, I would sit and stare at their pictures, still hanging on the walls of our home. I chose to sit in my pain and allow it to wash over me, a reminder that they had existed. I began looking at their friends, many of whom stayed in touch with me, vibrant young people who had gone on with their lives, found careers, traveled the world, played sports, and got engaged and married. My children would never experience these things. Much as I tried to be gracious and happy for their friends, I sometimes felt resentful about their successes. In time I would come to celebrate the lives others were living.

I often sat and imagined what might have become of Joshua and Leah's lives if they had not had Friedreich's Ataxia? What might they have been? Who would they have married? Would they have given me grandchildren? They should have outlived me. A parent should never have to bury their children. It went against the natural order of things even though there is, in reality, no natural order, just the chaos of life.

As much as I understood it, I was clearly experiencing post-traumatic stress disorder. I was in a deep state of mourning, mired in grief, missing my children, and looking at what I no longer had, not what remained. For all of my 57 years, I was an optimist, choosing only to see what was possible, not what I or my children could not do.

I began reading inspirational books about people who had overcome great challenges in their own lives. I was in a deep state of mourning, mired in grief, missing my children, and perhaps for the first time in my life, looking at what I no longer had, not what remained. Now I was in a very different place, wondering if I would ever feel happiness again or even be able to laugh again. I began reading books about people who had overcome great challenges in their own lives. Malala, the Pakistani girl shot in the face in retaliation for her activism on behalf of young women, who overcame her suffering and rose to great international prominence, the youngest person ever to win a Nobel Peace Prize. The most riveting story I read was "I'll Push You – Two Best Friends and One Wheelchair," by Patrick Gray and Justin Skeesuck, the story of a young man in a wheelchair who wanted to 'walk' the Camino, five-hundred miles over rough terrain and mountain passes. I had been there and was only able to walk one-hundred miles the first time. It was the most inspirational account of friendship, love, and endurance that I had ever read. I read the story of the Hoyt family, about a father and son completing the Ironman Triathlon in Hawaii. The father pulled his son in a dingy during the two-mile open-water swim, pulled him in a buggy behind his bike, and pushed his son in a specialized wheelchair while running to the finish line. I thought of the bravery of all of these people and of the amazing courage of my own children. They had all overcome so very much. If they could do it, so could I.

I was 60 as I entered the third year following Leah's death and I began to realize the only way to truly honor my children was to come back into life. As I had always been their devoted cheerleader, I now had to root for and believe in myself. I had to be my own champion. I was beginning to feel strong again and found myself celebrating their memory, remembering them laughing and talking without those memories triggering an emotional collapse. I was exhausted from my sadness and began focusing on trying to find joy in my life. When moments of sorrow came over me, I let them in, felt them, remembered my children in the best of times, and moved on. The heaviness slowly began to lift. I created a mantra for myself: "I want to reflect the courage, strength, and joy Joshua and Leah showed. Because of them I can do this!" I was determined not to let my suffering destroy me, but to consider it had somehow made me stronger. My children had shown me everyday life was for living and thriving, despite all the obstacles that stood in their way. This was their gift to me. I was slowly beginning to unwrap.

My wonderful "tribe," my longtime girlfriends, stayed in close contact with me. We met often for dinner, took long hikes around Puget Sound, kayaked, and enjoyed the great beauty of the Pacific Northwest. Being in nature, surrounded by life blooming amid dying trees and long-dead leaves, was restorative, gave me hope, and made me happy. Experiencing this was a reminder that life prevails, it miraculously finds a way to continue, even after a long, dark, cold winter. I needed to find a way to do just that. I began to dream again and created a long bucket list of things I wanted to experience and places I wanted to see. Having things to look forward to, helped me find joy, whether meeting up with friends or travelling to Africa, the Middle East or Europe.

Knowing I had done my best with my children, I began giving myself permission to focus on my own happiness and move forward without guilt. It was my time to be me and to do what I pleased. And in the years that followed I did exactly that—travelling the world and making sure I had all the experiences I yearned to live before I died.

I began planning trips to visit my family in Canada, and I decided the first goal I would tackle would be to go on safari and bungee jump in Zimbabwe, Africa. Just the thought of moving out in the world and forcing myself out of my comfort zone made me feel alive and stronger mentally and physically. As I took a dive off the bridge in Victoria Falls, I remember seeing a kayaker on the river below as I was falling. After I 'bounced' back up to the bridge I realized the kayaker was there as a safety net for any potential accidents. I was glad I did not consider that before I jumped, and I realized in that moment that there are always reasons to scare us away from testing our abilities and taking chances. Sometimes we can literally see the reasons that give us pause, but I think most of the time it is the fear in our minds that holds us back.

Traveling became my passion for several years and brought me back into life. I felt the presence of my children everywhere I went and would often see dragonflies, proof they were watching over me. I no longer cried when I thought about them. I just thought about the joy they had brought into my life. Sometimes I feel guilty enjoying my life as I thought the cost of my freedom was the fact that my children were gone, though I believe this is what they would want me to do. They would not want me to remain stuck and constantly mourning for them. Because I had spent my life with my children, helping them find joy, happiness, and purpose, I convinced myself it was my turn to do the same for me.

Though Cliff had encourage me to create my 'bucket list' and move forward with my life, he did not want to travel with me, preferring to stay home, hold down the fort, and take care of our little dogs, Sophie and Buddy. They were such a comfort to both of us, especially when we walked into our empty, quiet home. Their barks and wags always made me smile, and it made Cliff happy when they snuggled next to him as he watched television. He was happy to watch me come back to life and glad I was traveling with friends. He worried a bit about my safety because he knew I was an adventurer and a risk-taker, even more so since my children were gone. His concerns did not hold me back, and he did not want them to. It was my life, and both of us wanted me to live it on my terms.

I always knew I would walk the Camino again. I was not satisfied with the one hundred miles I had done with Leah's ashes, though I doubt, given the emotional burden following her loss, I could have done a longer journey. My first pilgrimage had given me many gifts: mostly the knowledge that I had fulfilled a promise I made to my daughter, but also the feeling that I could literally move forward with my life. I believed I could go even further this time. In January of 2017, I began planning my second walk for the following June. I would walk the entire five hundred miles from St. Jean-Pied-de-Port, France to Santiago, Spain and onward to Finisterra, Spain and the ocean. This pilgrimage would take five weeks, and again, I did not prepare physically by taking longer hikes at home. I felt ready. I knew better this time how to pack, and twelve pounds on my back was truly all I needed. I left behind excess baggage, such as snacks and extra clothing, and just packed the very minimum of what I would need. As I prepared for my second Camino, I thought about why I was doing this. Why did I need to put myself through this kind of challenge? The decision, in part, gave me a sense of purpose and direction, a reason for being alive. During my children's lives, there was never any question about my purpose. I had been living and breathing for Joshua and Leah. I realized that while I was always in the 'present' in the daily lives of my children, helping them with whatever they needed to get through their day, I was mostly preparing for future issues and challenges I knew would arise. I thought this long trek might help me to live fully in the moment, never an easy thing for me to do. I found a beautiful stone in the shape of a seashell at a shop near my home, a symbol of the Camino often shown along the way to direct traveler's footsteps. On the back of the shell were the words 'I Am Present.' I knew without a doubt this was a sign, a good omen I was on the right path. I tucked the stone into my pocket and decided in that moment I would not plan anything other than my travel arrangements. I would let each day bring whatever it might bring and again travel alone. I would walk with my thoughts and alongside other pilgrims on their own journeys, each with their own reasons, thoughts, and emotions. I knew from my first Camino I would never be truly alone. As it was my first time when I carried Leah's ashes, I knew I would again be part of a community of people, sharing meals, sipping wine, laughing and crying together, and sharing our stories. I knew I would be safe, both emotionally and physically. No one would care where you came from, what career you had, how much money you earned, the color of your skin, or what religion you practiced. I could be whoever I needed to be and as vulnerable as I needed to be. On the Camino, you are merely and miraculously a human being, in the company of strangers, yet deeply connected.

I arrived in St. Jean-Pied-de-Fort, France, on a very hot, muggy June day and felt excited to be there, filled with anticipation of what lay ahead. The little town was crowded with other pilgrims feeling as I did...happy, a little nervous, and ready to share stories. I checked into a small hostel and shared the room with a twenty-year-old girl I had met at dinner. It was her first Camino, and we talked about why we were walking. She was in her 'gap year,' preparing to go to university and looking for adventure. I was walking to try and learn how to stay 'present' and not live in a state of anticipating or worrying about the future. The next day I joined other pilgrims as we took the first steps on our five-hundred-mile journey. A beautiful sentiment spoken to greet one another along the way was "Buen Camino," meaning "have a great walk." This was said every time you met, passed, or walked away from another pilgrim.

I left at dawn and immediately began the very steep and already hot three-hour climb to Orrison where I stopped for breakfast and a water refill from a hose. I continued the climb to Roncesvalles for a total of twenty-seven kilometers and stayed at a large hostel where one hundred other pilgrims had stopped for the night. The initial trek over the Pyrenees Mountain range into Spain was arduous to say the least. There was a heat wave settling over Europe with temperatures over one hundred degrees. On the first two days of the walk, I was exhausted and dehydrated and began to have a little doubt about whether I could do this. I saw many people stop on the side of a very steep mountain incline, looking for shade, but there was none. The sun was beating down on all of us, and I was grateful I had brought along a 'cooling cloth' that held cold water for several hours as I draped it around my neck. There were stops along the way where we were able to refill our water bottles and have a bite to eat. During those two excruciating days, I was reminded of the physical challenges my children had faced almost every day of their lives, and the memory of their bravery helped me keep moving one foot in front of the other. I stopped at the occasional rest spots in the shade and watched people take off their shoes and bandage their toes together to keep blisters from rubbing against each other. Thankfully, I had no blisters this time, only very tired legs. The pain in my legs helped keep me focused and reminded me to stay in the 'present' and know that somehow, everything would work out. I walked with several young people, mostly from Europe, who were walking the Camino during their 'gap year' between high school and college as a way, they said, to think about what they wanted to study in college and what they wanted to do with their lives. A couple from the United States was recently retired, transitioning from their busy work lives and finally having the time to do this. Watching their body language as we walked and talked, I thought perhaps their marriage was also at risk, and perhaps other things were about to change for them. It seemed as if every pilgrim around me had remarkable stories to tell and compelling reasons to be on the Camino. No one seemed to there without purpose. Everyone seemed to be facing or processing extraordinary events in their lives. Few, if any, had come just to take a long, carefree walk.

The first major city my fellow pilgrims and I walked into was Pamplona, where in a couple of weeks they would celebrate the running of the bulls. I decided to stay for an extra night and enjoy the city, along with several new friends from Germany. The tapas and delicious aroma of foods like pulpo (octopus) in little outdoor pubs and cafés were such a welcome delight. I loved the chit-chat and relaxed atmosphere of this city and found my way to Ernest Hemingway's favorite bar for a glass of wine. Two weeks into the journey we made it through the mountain pass. I met a young man from Korea who told me he was deeply depressed and had contemplated suicide after many failures in his life. He had studied hard through his teenage years but had been rejected from all the universities to which he had applied. He was ashamed he was unable to provide for his widowed mother and believed he had been a huge disappointment to his family. As we walked to-gether, I told him my story of loss and grief and about my own struggle to find a way to move forward. Though his English was very limited and my Korean non-existent, we were some-how able to communicate our shared, painful experiences. He told me he was thankful I shared my story and that he had met someone older who had survived an almost insurmountable tragedy. We crossed paths several times over the next couple of weeks and always greeted each other as old friends, with hugs and smiles as we continued talking. I began to realize the reasons I was on this second Camino: to find purpose again in my life by reaching out, listening, and trying to help and inspire others. I visited him and others I had met in Korea a couple of years later and was happy to see he had found his way past his depression. We have stayed in touch over the years, and he recently married a beautiful young woman. This connection with strangers who became friends would happen many times over the next five weeks as I reached out to people who became almost instant friends, and my purpose was becoming clearer with each passing day. My story could help encourage and inspire others. The inspiration signs along the way reflected the deep feelings I had along the Camino.

"The spiritual pilgrimage begins with the feet and ends where the mind and the soul meet. From here our conscience penetrates the entire universe."

"Embrace the change coming your way. Explore, dis-cover, reach, and risk. Change creates energy inside of you that you did not realize you had."

And my personal favorite, a saying from J.R.R. Tolkien from *The Fellowship of the Ring.*

"All who wander are not lost."

We were all wanderers, but few seemed lost. We were all searching for something...on a quest for answers to often complicated questions, for the sustenance of being in a community of fellow traders. I met a beautiful young woman in an unhappy marriage and likely destined for divorce. I had been in her shoes many years earlier and felt an immediate connection to her. We walked and talked for several days. I listened closely as she told me about her struggles with anxiety and how she was not happy in her life. There was a moment when I felt compelled to give her my stone, the shell with the words 'I Am Present' carved into it. As I handed it to her, she began to sob and could feel my love and support.

"I know you feel broken, so I won't tell you to have a wonderful day. Instead I whisper these words to you: 'just hold on.' As the darkest days of grief start to get less, the sun will rise again for you."
- Zoe Clarke-Coates

Being present with her proved to be an amazing experience and allowed me to see an opportunity to reach out and touch someone who was in need. My eyes were opening more and more to my new purpose in life. Moments such as these helped keep me 'present' and taught me to pay more attention to what was happening in the moment. I reflected back for a little while, remembering how I always used to fill the quiet time with Leah, driven by a need to talk when all my daughter wanted was my presence and my silence. I was learning to be a better listener.

The more I walked forward, the more I realized I was really traveling inward. Five hundred miles over a five-week period seems like a long time, but to me, time and space had little importance. I just put one step in front of the other. My body was getting stronger, and after the first ten days I no longer felt any discomfort or fatigue, only the joy and newfound freedom of the journey. And not even a single blister. At the end of each day, I filled a tub with very cold water, soaked my feet, and took time to sit and reflect on the day. I thought about who I had met and about their stories, and as I reflected on the lives of my children, I was happy and imagined them watching over me and smiling.

Another person I met was a young man from Germany who had received a basketball scholarship to university. He had prepared for this his entire life, but a very serious injury to his knee changed everything for him. He was devastated and had no idea what to do next. His feet were incredibly blistered, as was his heart and soul, and I found myself 'over-caring' for him as a mother would perhaps do. We walked along with others, on and off for a couple of weeks, and I could see that although I thought I was being helpful, I was smothering him and he was becoming resentful. It was another gift of the Camino. Just because my heart is in the right place does not mean my actions are always appreciated. I thought about how my children sometimes told me to stop hovering and trying to control everything. I knew they were right, as I knew this young man was. It was a humbling truth I had to accept about myself and learn to step away when not invited, no matter how good my intentions are.

After thirty-five days, I arrived at Santiago, the final destination of the pilgrimage. My physical body was tired, but all the aches and pains I had felt along the way had subsided, and I felt like a warrior. I had accomplished something I was not certain I could do, and as I entered the cathedral at Santiago Square, quiet, happy tears poured down my face. The sun was shining, and I looked around at dozens of other happy, grateful warriors who, like me, could not believe they had 'walked the walk.' We were all changed and, I am certain, all transformed in different ways. A group of about ten of us, of every color, religion, and age, gathered on our final night with a deep understanding that the end of the Camino was the beginning of our new lives. We were going home to many different countries but with a shared commitment to take the gifts from our journey back with us.

I walked on with a couple young people for another one hundred miles to the ocean at Finisterra. I thought about the last time I was at this hallowed place just a few years earlier with Leah's ashes. Along with a fellow traveler, we looked for the lighthouse and the wooden cross where I had placed some of her remains and a few mementos, but they were no longer there. I was sad but also felt renewed and refreshed and believed that now I could move forward in my life. I watched as a dragonfly whooshed around me and took that as a sign from Leah that her spirit was with me. I felt a sense of peace I did not ever remember feeling in my life. I had survived a very difficult life, always bracing for the next crisis, worrying about whether my children were happy, trying to think up new adventures and activities that would keep them occupied. Now, standing by the water, I came into the present moment and realized that my previous life was over. It was time to acknowledge that.

I returned home after an incredible, thirty-seven-day, six-hundred-mile walk. I wanted to create a beautiful place for the remainder of my children's ashes so they could be close to me. My neighbor, Oksana, offered to help me build a flower garden next to a large, rose-colored cherry tree near my front door, and I buried them in that sacred place. Over the years, friends have donated small figurines and ornaments – dragonflies, butterflies, and caterpillars – to celebrate my children.

I walked the Camino again in July of 2018, with my friend Veronika from Slovenia whom I had met on my previous walk. We started in Lisbon, Portugal, and would end our journey once again in Santiago, Spain. This time I went to celebrate me...my life, my relationships, my journey through both the wonderful, magical, and very, very tough times I had survived. My 'mantra' was, "I want to be a reflection of the courage, strength, and joy that my children showed me and, because they demonstrated all of those traits, passed them on to me. This was a new route for me – the Portuguese Way – a newer pilgrimage and one that was easier to walk and far less crowded. As soon as I crossed over into Spain, walking through the forests and along the rivers and creeks, I began to feel peaceful as a calm washed over me, a sense of tranquility I had experienced on my previous journeys as I got closer to Santiago. After a long and sometimes difficult sixteen-day walk, we flew from Santiago to her hometown in Slovenia where I met her beautiful family and enjoyed a week of rest and more excellent food. I had learned the value of not missing out on opportunities and had to say "yes" when she invited me. I then returned home, happy and refreshed. I had focused on celebrating my life and felt a sense of joy and contentment. And perhaps more importantly, I felt a sense of significance, something I needed all of my life, as important to me as the air I breathe.

I was ready once again to give back and start volunteering. I wanted to use my life and experiences in any way I could to help others. I was rediscovering my 'significance' in life, a sense of purpose I had always needed. After Leah's death, I had stayed away from anything having to do with either her or Joshua's disease. I could not bear to deal with that, but now I was ready to reconnect and pay it forward. I began volunteering with the Make-A-Wish Foundation, the group that had been so generous with my children when our family needed a boost. I volunteered at the local foodbank too, another incredibly important organization that helped all three of us in our darkest moments. I started speaking at fundraising events including the Summit Assistant Dog Organization, the very one that had given Leah her beloved service dog, Bella. Through all of these efforts, I met many families who were going through the challenges of raising children with special needs and met parents who had also lost their children. I engaged with many of them, encourage them to have hope and belief that they could and would survive their pain. I was living proof of that and assured them they were not alone.

I planned to walk the Camino one more time in the summer of 2019, but I broke my foot playing racquetball in January. By June, I felt unsteady and was unsure if I could manage the arduous walks up steep trails and down mountain slopes. I loved all of my walks and hoped to continue every year for many years to come. It was like returning home every time I went back. This time I felt I was walking to listen. I seriously contemplated carrying a sign that indicated, *"I am not speaking today, only listening. Please feel free to share your story."* I felt that I needed to get better at listening without offering words of wisdom or feeling the need to fix others. I woke up and three in the morning on the eve of my departure, in the midst of having a panic attack, only the second one I had ever had in my life. I was hot and sweaty all over my body, and I could barely breathe, as though I were drowning. I was packed and ready to go, but the hour before I was to head to the airport, with tears in my eyes, I told Cliff I was not going. I was uncertain where this doubt was coming from but felt I needed to listen to my instincts, and I had an instant sense of relief after making the decision to stay home – a sure sign that it was the right thing to do.

It occurred to me that, whatever prompted my doubt about going on the Camino again, it was one of the few times in my adult life I recalled making a decision without having to consider anyone but me. Since my children's births and especially following their diagnoses, every decision, every thought, and almost every action had been made considering how it would affect them or my husband. I had been inextricably bound to Joshua's and Leah's needs and grateful for those connections, but now I was free to be whatever and whoever I needed to be. I had always had doubts about who I would be after their deaths, but I had discovered, after hundred of miles of walking, thinking, and praying, that I was, indeed, someone with knowledge, love, and vast experience I needed to share. I was a woman of significance and purpose.

Africa

Cambodia

Africa

Oman

A few years after both Leah and Joshua had passed, I learned from a relative that Keith, now 60, had died of Lou Gehrig's disease. It was oddly similar to the disease our children had in the way it progressed, but for Keith, the illness came on suddenly and he died less than two years after contracting it. I had not stayed in touch but decided I needed to bring closure to the anger and negative thoughts I was still feeling towards him.

Being there, seeing his urn with his picture next to it, I realized how much resentment I had been holding onto for too many years, feelings I never seemed able to shake. Sitting in the room, I realized it was now past time to let it all go. He was gone and holding onto any of that bitterness and resentment was only hurting me. I released my bad feelings and acknowledged that Keith had done the best he could as a husband and father. He had also grieved for his children and it was time for me to accept all that had transpired between us and move forward.

CHAPTER 16

The Gift of Great Sorrow

"Tell me the story of the mountain you climbed. Your words could become a page in someone else's survival guide."

—Morgan Harper Nichols

Eleven years have now passed since Joshua's death and eight years since Leah passed away and I am now 63. As I reflect on my life, especially in the wake of the loss of my children, I wonder whether it was worth writing this book and reliving my past, a past I would never change even if I could, but one filled with both great joy and immense suffering. To write the truth of our lives together and almost uncountable challenges we faced as a family required opening deep wounds, thinking about things I never allowed myself to consider, and confronting long-buried emotions. Was it worth the effort and could it possibly help anyone who has suffered terrible loss and pain? I must have believed both those things to be true, because I wrote our story.

I remember so many people who walked this improbable and unimaginable journey with us, and how they have shared with me the profound impact my family had on their lives. Our story helped many of them confront and talk about their own pain and grief, and they told me my honesty in sharing how I managed to move forward in my life helped them do the same.

I cannot even count the number of friends, family, and even casual acquaintances who told me I needed to write this book. Though I agreed I needed to take that step, I was, frankly, afraid to look back. Since my children were born and especially after their diagnoses, I was always very much a forward-thinking person. Looking back was never something I had time to do. Now, finally, I had time. I have discovered that the things that drive me in life are "purposefulness" and "meaningful interaction with people".

My purpose and hope in writing this book is that others will be empowered and inspired to believe they are stronger than they ever believed possible. Here is what I know: Time does soften the pain...that after initial grief and no matter how long that may last, happiness can return. Ultimately joy and positivity are choices. They do not just happen. My children taught me this, and I doubt I would have learned that lesson except for them.

Joshua and Leah both knew their lives would be short and they would, inevitably, die young. They had dreams as most young people do...that they would grow up, go away to college, fall in and out of love, find the right person, get married, and have children. They also knew those things would likely never happen. Still, they never gave up their hopes and dreams. They lived every day as if it were their last and found joy in the little things.. They managed to live full lives even when they were bedridden and in their last days. They talked about the things they would do when they were better, healed, and cured even though that was never going to happen for them. They kept talking about the future. Their faith held them steady and they believed, even in the waning days of their lives, they had a purpose.

One of the greatest gifts they gave me was the lesson that every day of our lives, even with the inevitable struggles, is a precious gift and not to be wasted. They taught me to keep making plans every day for the future we wanted to have. To live our best life no matter the circumstances. Anything can happen at any moment to anyone, and living in that fear only paralyzes us and doesn't allow us to live fully. We may have to shift our plans in a moment's notice, but still, we must make plans and move forward daily. Joshua and Leah, from the time they were young children, had scant-few easy days. I am in awe of the courage and joy they showed despite how hard life was for them, how they were able to love so freely, honestly, and openly. It was always my nature to have fun, laugh, and try to find joy whenever and wherever I could. I managed to do that even with, and perhaps because of, the challenges my children faced. Watching them find happiness despite the obstacles they faced taught me I could do anything.

I have been asked many times if I felt any guilt about passing-on the gene that resulted in their diagnoses. I never for a second felt guilt about that. It was something over which I had no control, so I never took that on. There was no way either their father or I could have known this terrible and fatal disease lurked somewhere far back in our familial DNA. I passed that on to Joshua and Leah unknowingly, but also believe I passed-on something else and perhaps something of even more importance...how to handle the life we have been given and in the best way we can.

Another one of the gifts I received from being a mother to Leah and Joshua is the gift of self-awareness. I recognize the years of care and love I gave them and am now, in the wake of their passing, able to embrace my own needs and take care of myself. It took me some time to realize this was self-care and not selfish. I also realized it was not someone else's responsibility to make me happy and that I was responsible for taking whatever time I needed to restore and fill my soul and, yes, find a way to be happy again. I'm learning how important it is to be kind to myself and to give myself the same grace that I would offer to others. If you are a caregiver reading this book, I hope you will take these words to heart and give yourself the care you need and deserve.

Whether we are caregivers to our children or our aging parents, if we do not stay healthy and occasionally break from the daily grind we risk becoming more resentful and less helpful to those for whom we care. I remember telling my children when I first took a vacation away from them how critical self-care was, how important it was to help maintain the happiness in our home and my ability to care for them. They were not happy about it and I took some verbal bashing as I was accused of being selfish. They were not always confident when I left that they would be okay without me since I was with them almost all day every day of their lives.

But, as things turned out, my short trips were good for me and them. It gave them confidence they could manage for short times just fine without their mother. I remember wondering *"what if something happens to me, how would they survive?"* I needed to ensure they and I knew without a doubt they would be okay. Their eventual acceptance of my need to get away and the confidence my absence gave them were gifts we gave each other. As they grew older, my children encouraged me to take time for myself whenever I needed it. They had become confident that they would be fine without me and they could see how I would return with a lighter heart and more joy in my spirit.

As I was raising my children I became more aware it was my faith in God that got me through the challenges we all faced. Everyone confronts difficulties and pain in their lives. I see now it was my faith in God sustaining, guiding, and allowing me to go through my journey without anger, resentment, or bitterness. It is by the grace of God I stand in this place today, still a woman of faith, happy and grateful for the time I had with Joshua and Leah. I have always had faith that God knows what He is doing. How could He not? You know the often-used phrase *"God doesn't give us more than we can handle,"* a phrase I have always disliked. My response when people would say that to me was, *"I wish He didn't have so much confidence in me."* Apparently, though, He did. I felt honored God believed I could handle this and honored I was chosen to be the mother of my remarkable children. My children's own faith in me proved I could deal with very tough stuff. They were living proof . I was chosen to be their mother, I was strong, resilient, and able to help them live their very best lives. Another gift of self-awareness. Throughout their lives, I was on a journey into the unknown, not aware or even believing I could do it, but, somehow, I did.

Expecting life to return to "normal" after a traumatic loss is unrealistic and can lead to great disappointment. You can get stuck in the past and it can hold you back from moving forward. I would ask myself "when will I feel like my old self again?" I had to learn that the sadness would never truly leave and I would have to reframe my ideas of what joy would look like. I had to create a "new normal" that would, over time, co-exist with the sadness in my heart and help me live a full and satisfying life.

I will miss Joshua and Leah every day for the rest of my life. Whenever I see a dragonfly, it always puts a smile on my face because I feel Leah's presence around me. When I hear rap music or anything about the word of God – even when someone says, "God bless you!" – I feel Joshua's presence. Loss is expressed when something cannot be found. Our loved ones leave us with an imprint of themselves that lives on in us. We never truly loose them.

Thinking about them almost always brings tears to my eyes because I wonder what they would be doing had they been given more years to live. I do not miss the difficulty of our everyday lives. Seeing your children struggle to do the basic things most of us take for granted was agony for us all. I wanted to take away their pain and put it in my own body. That was a power I did not possess so I used the only power I had, helping them live their best lives. It comforts me knowing they are no longer suffering, but instead running around the gates of Heaven and no doubt raising a little hell.

Believing there is life after death also gives me comfort, the thought I may be with them again someday, out of their wheelchairs, and free of the constraints they faced when they were alive here on Earth. I also believe they are watching over me, loving me, proud of their mother, and very much wanting me to live my own best life. Another gift, their way of saying "thank you" for taking care of us.

I have been asked if I would have switched my children for healthy ones. The honest answer to that hypothetical question is two-fold. I would have loved for Joshua and Leah to be healthy. What parent would not want that for their kids? The other part of the answer is I would not have traded them for anything. They gave me the opportunity to be a better person, a completely devoted mother, a less selfish human being, and a person who had to reach deep inside herself to find out exactly how tough she truly was. Joshua and Leah made me stronger than I ever thought possible, a woman able to *"pick herself up, brush it off, and keep going."* I had learned the hard truth of this as a child but now I saw it as the gift it truly was. Another gift.

My mantra has become "No Regrets." For me grief was so much more difficult to walk through because I had regrets about Leah. To this day I regret missing the signs of Leah's eventual diagnosis and believing she was acting-out to get attention. I regret the time I did not spend understanding my daughter. I regret I did not invest as much energy into her as I did her brother. I still live with a deep sadness about that. The gift in it now is I make choices that will not leave me with feelings of regret.

My children's lives and deaths have made me a more compassionate, less judgmental, and more empathic person. When people meet and look at me, they could never guess what I have experienced. This makes me realize when I look at someone, I cannot possibly know who they are or what they have gone through in their own lives. Because of that knowledge, the realization of what I do not and cannot know allows me to give people grace and show kindness to them. My own suffering has made me more conscious of the importance of not making assumptions about other people. I learned how much the little things gave Joshua and Leah, a smile, kind word or gesture, ability to take a walk or, quite literally, to smell the roses. After they passed, I tried daily to practice giving the little things to both friends and strangers. Joshua especially had the gift of always seeing the best in others. I remember that and try as best I can to be like him. Another gift from my children.

Even more, one of the greatest gifts they have given me is the importance of not taking a single day for granted, living in the moment, and finding the small treasures in everyday life. Joshua and Leah knew their lives would be short so they made the best of every day. None of us really knows when we will take our final breath, but we should live as they did, fully and happily, aware our days are always numbered. I am grateful for my good health, for the freedom I have in this country, for the ability to take a walk on a sunny day or even a rainy day, frequent here in the Pacific Northwest. As I appreciate a smile from a stranger, I always make eye contact and smile as I pass someone on my walks. I nod hello and try to make each person whose path I cross feel as if they have been noticed. I try to make them feel significant, a feeling I have always needed. Like my children, I have learned to ask for help when I need it and to give compliments when people might not expect them. I always remember how Joshua would tell girls how beautiful they were even though he was blind. He would speak from his heart and light up their faces. Another gift.

If Joshua and Leah were sitting across from me today, I would thank them for giving me the gift of being their mother, the mother they needed for their time here. I would tell them they lived their lives with honor, integrity, purpose, love, and joy, and remind them how many people around the world they touched and inspired.

And my final words to them would be simply, "Well done, my babies, well done!"

The story I have shared in these pages is neither more nor less painful than anyone else's. I just wanted to share my truth... I believe there are gifts in every loss we endure, whether a beloved spouse, dear pet, or even one's children. It often takes time and deep reflection to unwrap them and has taken me years to discover what Joshua and Leah gave me and to almost every person they knew.

As I told my son long ago when he asked if he was going to die. We don't know when or how we will die, only God knows that. Our job is to figure out our purpose on this Earth and how to live the best life as God intended.

That answer was good enough for him and for me now. I hope I have a lot of life left and I contemplate how I want to be remembered when it is my time to go. Now when I face new challenges in whatever time remains, I ask myself, "How can I face this and live the very best life possible?"

And then I take the plunge.

Remembrances –
Where Immortality Lives

The purpose of life is not to be happy. It is to be useful, to be honorable, to be compassionate, to have it make some difference that you have lived and lived well".
—Ralph Waldo Emerson

From Tammi Swenson Booth, Caregiver

"The first thing I noticed when I applied for the caregiver position with Joshua and Leah was their wheelchairs. They were both young teenagers and I felt overwhelmed, unsure how to transfer them and not drop them. I felt an instant connection with Louise who became like a mom to me. I was only 21 and initially thought she was being too picky about how things needed to be done. I thought she was being selfish when she wanted to be away from the kids for a while. Now with children of my own, I see how vitally important that time

away was for her. Most parents need a break when their children are in optimum health and able to live independently from their parents as they grow older. With special-needs kids, time away is even more important. Louise taught me the importance of self-care and that it was not at all about being selfish, but about recharging one's body and soul to be a better parent. Louise was an amazing mother. Amazing. She was the perfect mother for the children she saw as perfect, even when the world did not see things that way. Whenever I meditate and think about gratitude, Joshua is the first person who comes to mind. He thanked me for every little thing I did for him. And I will always carry that memory of him with me for the rest of my life."

From Jessie Graham Chapman, Caregiver

"When I began caring for Joshua and Leah I felt very comfortable. I had been around family and friends with special needs my whole life. I became more of a sibling than a professional caregiver, and my bond with the entire family became strong. Louise told me from the beginning that my primary purpose was to bring laughter and fun into Joshua and Leah's lives while also helping to care for their physical needs. We went shopping, to sports events, to the Puyallup Fair and did many other social activities with their friends. I learned to NEVER take a moment for granted, to endeavor to live my best life and to smile, especially around people having a bad day. Each one of us has the potential to make a positive impact in the world. It's a choice."

From Jessyca Swatman, Caregiver

"It was an honor to care for Leah and Joshua and watching Louise love and care for these very special children made me a better mom. The time I spent with them gave me a different view of life and I saw that we are all people with different needs and abilities, some more visible than others, but a common

thread that bind us to one another. I loved being in their home and I always said I wanted to be adopted by Louise. It felt so good knowing she trusted me with her precious children and I felt like a daughter to her and a sister to Joshua and Leah. It was inspiring to see them overcome their many challenges and to help them find ways to do that. It was great fun to plan 'normal' teenage activities with them...going to parties, school dances, and even trips to the state fair. We made so many beautiful memories together that will live forever in my heart. Though losing them was the most painful and emotionally draining experience of my life, I would do it all over again."

From Brianne Sembar, Caregiver

"Being Joshua's and Leah's caregiver and spending time in their home and in their environment completely changed me. In truth, I hated my life before them. I did not like who I was and caring for them gave my life purpose and meaning. Fourteen years later, following their deaths, I am still a caregiver for special needs people because of what I learned being with them. As I was helping them and Louise, they were all saving my life. I wanted to give up and felt as if I had no life inside me. I felt totally accepted in their family and it was far more than a job to me. It was a calling and still is to this day. I am able to work with a variety of people because of the experiences I had with them. They taught me so much about strength, courage, and compassion and I became a better human being. They opened my eyes and made me feel worthy of their love and, in doing that, taught me to love myself... something I never thought I could do. They showed me how I

brought value to them. On many, many days, the hugs I got from Louise, Joshua, and Leah were the only reason to get up in the morning. Their physical touch meant more to me than they ever knew.

"Joshua had a wonderful sense of humor and could light up a room just by entering it. The love he had for Jesus was palpable and radiated out to all of us who were lucky enough to be in his presence. It was truly amazing to watch this young man transform himself from a lost and angry teenager into a man of God. Knowing they are both in the arms of our creator made losing them a little bit easier. Leah was one of the most beautiful people I have ever known...inside and out. I loved being around her. Despite the physical challenges she faced, she never showed defeat, just kept on going and thriving in everything she did. She taught me humility and that while we cannot control the things that happen to us in life, we can control our perspective and how we react to them. We were often just a bunch of crazy kids, driving around in their minivan, listening to their favorite music. We would sometimes hang out at the mall and often lose Joshua if we turned away from him for just a minute. Leah would shake her head because she knew he was somewhere getting himself in trouble. Most of the time she was right. I would hold the memories of our time together until we meet again."

From Julie Braün, Louise's sister

"You cannot understand the fullness of Joshua and Leah's life without knowing their mom, my sister Louise. Growing up with my sister Louise is like attending a master class in 'Embracing Possibilities!' From our younger years to the present, Louise has paved the way on a journey of discovery, experiences, and gathering people. She lives her life by a couple of fundamental mottos that kept things interesting: 'where there's a will, there's a way' and '"the rules are for other people.' Little did we know how well these would serve her. She *has a thirst for adventure and will not be left behind. She may, or may not have FOMO, a fear of missing out. It's not an option. Throughout our lives she has had an abundance of great ideas and advice that she has willingly shared and of which I have been the gracious recipient. I always feel special when I'm with Louise, like I am a gift to her. It's her superpower. Josh and Leah touched people in a way that made them unforgettable, not because of their disability...unforgettable because of the spirit they exuded. Their smile, style, and easy laughter made you want to be a part of the magic that was Joshua and Leah. Amazing things happened when they were around. Neither Joshua, Leah, nor Louise ever surrendered to the challenges they faced and when I think I cannot do something or face some obstacle, I think of the three of them and I keep going forward."*

From Andrew Farnham, Joshua's best friend

"Joshua and Leah taught me how precious times is with friends and all of the people you love. I learned how to be reliable and loyal and that every moment matters whether it is a birthday, holiday, or the one-hundredth sleepover.. I learned the difference between empathy and sympathy and how to listen and acknowledge when something is hard instead of trying to see only a silver lining. I learned how to process grief after my lifelong friends passed away and how to be sensitive with others who are grieving their own losses. Friendship is precious...the greatest gift from Josh and Leah."

From "Auntie" Wanda Pratt

"It was an honor to be a longtime friend and part of this family and to be trusted to come and care for Joshua and Leah when Louise needed to have some time to herself to recharge her emotional batteries. Joshua taught me to be aware of and connect to my spirit, the very essence of people. After he could no longer see, he told me once when I visited that he knew it was me because of the color he saw when I entered the room.

It was the color purple. While others may have judged him, he lived without judgment of others. Leah was my girl and I loved to spoil her. She taught me the importance of compassion, a deeply caring, but pragmatic girl. Hers was a quieter faith than her brother's, but she was deeply spiritual nonetheless. More than anything, I loved how she let me love her. I will love and remember both of these magical children every day of my life. And let me take a moment to honor and extol their mother, who never discussed the fact that her babies were leaving a little bit at a time. Watching how she managed their lives and never gave in to their disease taught me to focus on how to live life to the fullest."

ACKNOWLEDGEMENTS

First and foremost, I want to thank my two precious children, Joshua and Leah, the most beautiful gifts I have ever received. I did not choose to have children with special needs, but I believe they chose me, and I am forever blessed by that. I want to thank them for being so incredibly brave throughout their too-short lives and giving me a sense of purpose in caring for them. You both set a beautiful example of how each of us can live our best life no matter the obstacles we face, and you inspired everyone you met to choose a better path for their life. I am a better person because of you.

My gratitude for my husband Cliff is immeasurable. You took a risk in marrying me, not knowing what you were heading into, but you took me and the kids on anyway and stayed with us throughout our journey. You have been by my side for more than 20 years and an anchor when I felt the waves pulling me under. Your quiet strength, support, and love have been and continue to be my safe haven.

Thank you to my mother, Marie-Paule Boulianne, and my father, Marcel Braün, for the lessons you taught me throughout my childhood; lessons, though sometimes painful, that gave me the strength and confidence I needed to survive an unexpected and challenging life.

My siblings Pierre, Denise, Nicole, Julie, and Rene gave me much love, humor, and support all the years we grew up together. When I was a little girl, I hoped to be just like you!

I'm especially grateful for my little sister Julie, her

husband Glen, and their three daughters, Sarah, Rachel, and Ariane (my schmoopies). You have always been in my corner and welcomed me into yours. You have embraced my free spirit and accepted me as I am, flaws and all.

There is no way I could have managed the day-to-day care of Joshua and Leah without the help of Tammi Swenson Booth, Jessyca Swatman Turner, Jessi Graham Chapman and Brianne Sembar Denton, our compassionate and quirky and fun loving caregivers. You gave Joshua and Leah the gift of living "normal" lives and brought fun, laughter, and craziness into our lives. You gave me respite when I needed it and allowed me time to rest, rejuvenate, and care for myself so I could be a better mom.

Without my tribe – Alisa Kruse, Amy Jahn, April Alexander, Arlene Wolf, Cindy Herley, Debby Wells, Denise Braün Boisclair, Janet Farnham, Julie Braün, Marie-Noelle Nesbit, Nicole Braün Derrien, Tracy Godat, and Wanda Pratt (in alphabetical order of course because I wouldn't want any of you to imagine another being more important than you are

"When you find people who not only tolerate your quirks but celebrate them with cries of 'me too,' be sure to cherish them, because those weirdos are your Tribe!"

to me! lol!) I could not have survived the path I was traveling without all of you by my side. Through thick and thin, in sickness and in health, love and divorce, riches and poverty, joy and sadness, and life and death, you held me up and stood beside me. You saved me. We are forever bound. (Plus you all know too much about me so it's safer to keep you close. Lol!)

I would be remiss if I didn't take this moment to thank my dearest friend from Auburn, April Alexander for her love, laughter and tireless encouragement. We raised our children side by side and you literally walked through each phase of the writing of this book, put up with my constant questions, concerns, frustrations, successes and tears. When I couldn't think of the right words to say, you helped them flow and assisted with editing along the way. How many times did you have to talk me off the cliff and remind me how important this book would be. Our weekly dinner/movie nights at my home and all the other fun shenanigans, kept me sane and continue to be a highlight in my week.

I am so grateful for all my Camino friends who walked, talked, and listened alongside me. We shared laughter and tears and are all better for having walked those hundreds of miles together. Thank you for caring for my poor, blistered feet and showing me where the wine spigots were at the vineyards along the way.

I want to acknowledge and thank all the professional men and women who cared deeply for my children and gave them the gift of better health and more time. A special thank you to the physicians and entire medical staff at Seattle Children's Hospital and the Summit Assistant Dog program in Anacortes, Washington for the gift of Bella, Leah's beloved service dog. I am forever indebted to the Alaska Washington Make-a-Wish Foundation for creating beautiful memories for Joshua and Leah and our entire family. Thanks also to FARA, the Friedreich's Ataxia Research Alliance for your commitment to bringing-together the medical communities around the world to find treatments and a possible cure for FA.

I will be forever indebted to my children's teachers and special education staff for ensuring Joshua and Leah were more than just a statistic and helping enrich their lives in such special ways.

I want to thank Julie Blacklow, journalist and author, who believed from the first time we met that my story needed to be told. Your compassionate guidance throughout the writing process helped make this book possible. You made me go deep and then deeper into places I did not always want to go. You helped me turn my dream of telling my story into reality. I am certain Joshua and Leah would be saying, "Well done!"

I am also so grateful for the help and guidance of Gail Hudson, author and life coach, who helped me further expose the many gifts and teachings of my journey. From the first moment we spoke, you understood my passion for guiding others through the process of loss and grief and helped me bring out those teaching moments.

My special gratitude to Tracy Godat, Rick Bates, Julie Braun, Serge Timacheff, and Phil Johnson for your help with editing and photography. Your fingerprints are all over this book.

Finally, I would like to thank the staff at Atmosphere Press for believing in my story and helping bring it to publication. I hope this book helps you, reader, walk thru your journey from pain to purpose.

The "Joy Thru Tears Foundation" is a non-profit organization (501C3) created by Louise Braün Frank. They are passionate about honoring the love, dedication and tireless commitment caregivers provide to whomever they assist. Their mission is to offer a gift of self-care that will refresh and rejuvenate the caregivers' mind, body and spirit. Louise is available for speaking and book signing opportunities and is ready to share resources she found helpful during this most difficult time in her life. Her foundation is currently partnering with three primary charities:

- The Alaska Make-a-Wish Foundation
- Summit Assistance Dog Program in Anacortes, Washington
- FARA – the Friedreich's Ataxia Research Alliance.

Your donations and continued support are greatly appreciated.

Contact Louise at: www.JoyThruTears.Foundation
Or by email at: Louise.Frank@JoyThruTears.Foundation

Resources for information and support in coping with loss, grief and trauma

1. For information on Friedreich's Ataxia contact:
   FARA (Friedreich's Ataxia Research Alliance) at
   https://curefa.org
2. For information on the Summit Assistance Dog
   program contact:
   https://summitdogs.org
3. For information on Make A Wish Foundation
   contact:
   https://wish.org
4. For information and support after a child dies
   contact:
   www.compassionatefriends.org
5. For information and support after diverse types of
   grief contact:
   www.griefshare.org

The symptoms & rate of progression **vary.** Loss of balance and coordination is often noticed first.

Everyone has the FXN gene. Those with FA have a mutation which silences the FXN gene reducing the protein frataxin.

2 serious heart conditions, **CARDIOMYOPATHY** and **ARRHYTHMIA** can lead to early death.

Frataxin is essential to energy production.

Cognition is NOT AFFECTED

Many have aggressive scoliosis requiring spinal fusion surgery

What is Friedreich's Ataxia (FA)?

10%

of people with FA have **TYPE 1** DIABETES.

In the later stages of FA, patients experience loss of VISION, SPEECH & HEARING.

6 to 8 years after diagnosis most lose the ability to WALK unassisted.

ABOUT ATMOSPHERE PRESS

Atmosphere Press is an independent, full-service publisher for excellent books in all genres and for all audiences. Learn more about what we do at atmospherepress.com.

We encourage you to check out some of Atmosphere's latest releases, which are available at Amazon.com and via order from your local bookstore:

The Swing: A Muse's Memoir About Keeping the Artist Alive, by Susan Dennis

Possibilities with Parkinson's: A Fresh Look, by Dr. C

Gaining Altitude - Retirement and Beyond, by Rebecca Milliken

Out and Back: Essays on a Family in Motion, by Elizabeth Templeman

Just Be Honest, by Cindy Yates

You Crazy Vegan: Coming Out as a Vegan Intuitive, by Jessica Ang

Detour: Lose Your Way, Find Your Path, by S. Mariah Rose

To B&B or Not to B&B: Deromanticizing the Dream, by Sue Marko

Convergence: The Interconnection of Extraordinary Experiences, by Barbara Mango and Lynn Miller

Sacred Fool, by Nathan Dean Talamantez

My Place in the Spiral, by Rebecca Beardsall

ABOUT THE AUTHOR

Louise Braün Frank was born in Ottawa, Canada. Raised in a military family with five brothers and sisters, she moved many times in Canada and even had the opportunity to live in France. All those experiences cultivated her curiosity and passion for travel, though she never imagined the life she would live once she settled in the Seattle area. Louise's two children, Joshua and Leah, were both diagnosed when they were young with Friedreich's Ataxia, a rare, progressive, and debilitating disease which, over the course of their short lives, took away their abilities to walk, see, and hear. It is a disease with no cure and always fatal. The children, with the help of a determined and committed mother, outlived the doctor's predictions and both survived into their twenties. In addition to helping her children live their best lives, Louise built a successful direct sales business with the Pampered Chef and continues with that work today. She is also an advocate for volunteerism and gives her time to the Make-a-Wish Foundation and local food banks. In 2021 she created the Joy

Thru Tears Foundation to honor caregivers by giving a gift of self-care that will refresh and rejuvenate their mind, body, and spirit. Over the years since her children's deaths, she has been invited as a guest speaker to share her experiences with the hope it will inspire healing in others who have also suffered great loss, turning her pain into purpose. She has also walked the Camino in Spain on three different occasions, each time searching for and finding a way to grow spiritually and move forward in her life. She plans to go back again.

Made in USA - Kendallville, IN
38766_9781639882700
03.22.2022 1425